7/11/07
To Steve

May be
you as you re~
your mind —
Rom 12:1-2
Dr. Veith

A Slow Motion Miracle

by

Dr. Vick L. Newsom, D. Min.

Bloomington, IN   Milton Keynes, UK

AuthorHouse™
1663 Liberty Drive, Suite 200
Bloomington, IN 47403
www.authorhouse.com
Phone: 1-800-839-8640

AuthorHouse™ UK Ltd
500 Avebury Boulevard
Central Milton Keynes, MK9 2BE
www.authorhouse.co.uk
Phone: 08001974150

First published by AuthorHouse 5/15/2007

ISBN: 1-4208-6910-8 (sc)

Printed in the United States of America
Bloomington, Indiana

This book is printed on acid-free paper.

Table of Contents

Acknowledgements

I acknowledge the Holy Spirit of the living God as the inspiration for this book. Without His participation there would have been no "Slow Motion Miracles." This book is specifically for those who have made Jesus Christ the Lord and Master of their lives and have the Holy Spirit dwelling within them. Parts of it will work for those who are unsaved, but to realize the full power of this teaching, you must make Jesus your Lord and Master! *It is critical that you accept that God is sovereign and has the final say – If you have truly given your life over to Him you must learn to trust Him completely!*

I stand on the shoulders of many men and women of God who have shared their ideas with me though their books and radio programs. Their insights and observations have been invaluable in developing the counseling techniques presented in "A Slow Motion Miracle."

Please note that all the examples in this book are compilations of my experiences as a Christian counselor and no confidences are compromised. All names were changed to prevent any embarrassment to clients or their families.

This book is dedicated to the following: My blessed Savior, the Lord Jesus Christ first and foremost; also to my wonderful helpmate for over forty-three years, my wife Margy and my four terrific children, Victoria, Billy, Christopher, and Cylani Jane (CJ). How you all have made my life a grand and glorious experience. To my mother who is an inspiration to me, my friends, John and Lou Ann Warner (thanks for the great cover John) and Ron and Karen Nespeca who all reviewed this work tirelessly. Lastly to my clients who are the true heroes of "A Slow Motion Miracle."

Glory to God Counseling, LLC can be contacted at Dr.Vick@glorytogod.net or 417-334-8777

Our web site address is WWW.GlorytoGod.net

WARNING: I never recommend that a client discontinue any medication prescribed by a doctor as they go through this counseling methodology. It can be dangerous to discontinue medications without the agreement of your Doctor! As your situation improves, go to your Doctor and have him reevaluate your medication needs.

Preface

This is a book about hope and the provisions our loving heavenly Father has made for us to enjoy the love, joy, and peace discussed in the Scriptures. There is hope for you to change your life. It is based on the promises given to us in the most wonderful book ever written, the Bible.

A friend of mine, after reading this book, said that the miracles were anything but "slow." I think he is right. The changes that people make in their lives with the aid of the Holy Spirit are astounding. And they often occur in a very short period of time.

An analogy I use is this: You are paddling up the river of life with a strong current against you. You have a one horsepower paddle and are working as hard as you can, but losing control. Because you are a believer in Christ, sitting behind you in the boat is a 1000 horsepower engine waiting to be turned on. This engine is the Holy Spirit. You turn and smile at Him occasionally. But you never give Him permission to become involved in your struggle. My advice, invite Him to help you!

I encourage you to read this little book from cover to cover for a good understanding of the principles it contains. A good start to developing the "Christ-like" self-image in you is to answer everyone who asks you, "How are you?" with "I am blessed."

Chapter One

What is a Godly Self-Image?

Something to think about: If a person can knowingly continue committing a sin and not feel the conviction of the Holy Spirit for committing that sin, he may not have accepted Jesus Christ as his Lord and Savior.

In the mid 1960's Satan, in concert with the emerging "new age movement," launched an attack on the church with a discovery in "pop" psychology called self-improvement through positive confession. This was championed as a way to help you to be more who you wanted to be by changing your self-image. Self-image is what comprises your mental and spiritual concept of who you are and how you "see" yourself.

What the world had rediscovered was something God had told us about in the Bible thousands of years ago. Basically, whatever you think about and focus your mind on impacts in a dramatic way how your life unfolds. For instance, if you see yourself as popular and friendly, others will perceive you that way. On the other hand, if you see yourself in your mind's eye as a loser, no matter what you do to succeed, you will probably fail.

The Deceiver and the Deception

As with many things the devil brings to us, there is just enough truth in this "new" idea to make it appear to work. If you told yourself often enough that you were a great person, some of it would penetrate your subconscious mind and cause short-term changes to occur. This falls right into the hands of your enemy, Satan. What this "positive confession technique" leaves out is God and puts you in place of Him. This is idolatry in its purest form, where God is removed from the throne of your heart, and you place yourself there instead.

What Satan has done is take a true concept of God and corrupt it into an idolatrous act. What we must do as followers of Jesus Christ is revise the "positive confession technique" to place God on the throne of our heart. We then begin to develop the "Christ-like" self-image in us through confessing how God sees us as His children.

Godly Positive Confession and the Picture Album

So how do we go about using "positive confession" in a way that is pleasing to our heavenly Father? The place to start is to know for certain that you are one of His children. You cannot enjoy His blessings if you do not first have a relationship with Him through His Son, Jesus

Christ. Once that is established, the next step is to begin to understand a little of how wonderfully complex God has made you.

In simple terms, your mind is made up of two parts. About twenty percent is your conscious mind. This is where you make decisions such as what to wear, where to eat lunch and so on. The remaining eighty percent comprises your subconscious mind and it is like a giant video recorder storing pictures from birth until now. Once the pictures are stored in the subconscious a mechanism, called the "creative subconscious" by Lou Tice in his book "Smart Talk," begins to try to duplicate those pictures in your real life experiences.

The first twenty years of your life will have the most impact on your subconscious. Therefore the relationship you had as a child with your care givers is extremely important to your self-image. All the "pictures" you have in your subconscious combine to determine how you "see" yourself.

This self-image is your mental and spiritual concept of who you think you are. Many things have influenced this image as you have walked through life. Since you live in a fallen world with all of its evil influences, you have developed many destructive and incorrect photos and have placed them in the picture album in your subconscious mind. This is exactly what the enemy of your soul, Satan, wants you to do (Rev 12:10). These negative pictures make you less effective in your service to God.

Beginning today you will begin to learn what pictures your loving Father wants you to have in your subconscious photo album and how changing those pictures will make your life prosper and be in health as your soul prospers (3 John 1:2).

In *Psycho-Cybernetics,* Dr. Maxwell said that the self-image is the key to human personality and behavior. He believed it to be one of the most important discoveries of the twentieth century, and I agree. A great deal of your self-image is dictated by your subconscious mind, which is like a camera or a video recorder placing pictures in your mental picture album from the moment you are born. As you read this book you will begin to understand how to change your self-image in your internal picture album. You will change these pictures one at a time using the promises of the Word of God. Examples of the promises of God you should use to replace your negative confessions are:

- I have great value because God loved me enough to die in my place.

- People will like me because I treat them like they are my beloved brothers and sisters in the Lord.

- I succeed in what I attempt to accomplish because I have the Holy Spirit guiding my steps.

Your loving Father wants you to have photos in your subconscious picture album that will make your life prosper and be in health <u>as your soul prospers</u>.

3 John 1:2; Beloved, I pray that you may prosper in all things and be in health, just as your soul prospers.

Believers Living Defeated Lives

In the True Church (those who have accepted Jesus as their Savior and made Him Lord of their lives) only fifteen to twenty percent are living a free and productive life in Christ. All believers have settled their vertical relationship (they are going to heaven when they die) but their horizontal relationships with their family and others are a mess. I believe this is part of the reason that non-Christians see no reason to accept Jesus as Lord. We in the church have the same divorce rate, many of our children are out of control, we lie, steal and backbite along with the world, and we have the same mental illnesses. So why don't we look different?

How Do You "See" Yourself?

There is a direct relationship between your trust in the Word of God and your understanding of God's promises for you. The Holy Word living in your heart will determine what you will believe in your mind about how you "see yourself." The way you "see yourself" will determine the way your life unfolds. If you wish to change the outside, it is critical that you change the way you view yourself on the inside. To release your potential, you need to correct the misinformation that you have stored in your subconscious photo album. Don't accept the lies of Satan; accept what your heavenly Father says about you.

The Word - Logos and Rhema

The techniques I teach you in this book will enable you (with the help of the Holy Spirit) to change your worldly self-image to the Christ-like self-image. These techniques are all based on you speaking the Word of God to yourself so you can improve the way you "see" yourself. The Word of God must change from Logos to Rhema to be most effective for you.

So what is Logos? The entire Bible is the "Logos" or "Word" of God and is absolute truth without error. Our minds are designed by God to be like a sponge that absorbs the Scripture (Logos) you place in it. A way of "soaking up Logos" is to develop a set of cards that contain Scriptures. These Scriptures need to address issues that you need to change to improve your self-image. Once you have filled your mind with the Logos, the Holy Spirit can transform the Logos into Rhema.

So what is Rhema? Rhema is when Scripture you have stored in your mind becomes "alive" to you. It is as if the Holy Spirit squeezes the sponge of your mind that contains the Logos and begins changing it into Rhema. The Holy Spirit will apply it directly to the transformations you need to make in your self-image. This will help you develop the Christ-like self-image you desire.

The comparison of Logos and Rhema is that Logos is like a jackhammer changing your photos one piece at a time. Rhema is like a stick of dynamite that will affect a much quicker change to the subconscious picture album.

Remember that you cannot get Rhema without Logos in your mind, just like you cannot get water from a dry sponge.

Godly Self-Talk

It is vital that we control the thoughts of our heart/mind by the use of godly self-talk and visualization of the desired goal.

Matt. 12:36-37; "For out of the abundance of the heart the mouth speaks. A good man out of the good treasure of his heart brings forth good things, and an evil man out of the evil treasure brings forth evil things."

It is important to understand that when the Scriptures use the word "heart," it often refers to the mind. These two words, heart and mind, are used interchangeably in many places in the Word of God.

Please note that the godly self-talk and visualization I am referring to is not the same as what the new age and eastern religions refer to in their teachings. Their teachings are, in the best case, humanistic and can be potentially demonic. Any visualization or self-talk that does not emphasize the Word of God and His love for you is too be avoided.

Even scripturally correct teaching will not automatically clear up the wrong ideas you have about God's desire to bless you. The problem is, even scripturally correct truth cannot always penetrate a self-image that is filled with misinformation about who you are in Jesus Christ. You need to understand what your rights and privileges are because you are a child of God. For example if you pour pure water through a contaminated filter, the water will come out polluted and unhealthy. It is the same when you filter God's truth through concepts that are incorrect.

As children of the King, it is vital that all your desires be in line with the great commandment: "Love God and Love your fellow man." You cannot truly love others until you understand how much our Heavenly Father loves you and wants you to succeed.

Only one person had a perfect self-image and that was the Lord Jesus, who was God made flesh and dwelt among us.

John 1:14; "And the Word became flesh and dwelt among us, and we beheld His glory, the glory as of the only begotten of the Father, full of grace and truth."

Jesus, who was fully God and fully man, was tempted in every way we are but He did not have our "sinful nature." He was therefore able to develop only godly pictures to go into his human picture album. You, as a child of the King and joint heir with Christ, have the ability to change your self-image. You can develop the "Christ-like" self-image and begin to look more like Jesus every day.

Rom. 8:16-17; "The Spirit Himself bears witness with our spirit that we are children of God, and if children, then heirs—heirs of God and joint heirs with Christ, if indeed we suffer with *Him,* that we may also be glorified together."

Progressive Sanctification or "Changing Your Pictures"

The accepting of Jesus as your Savior is called "justification." The next step in your walk with the Lord is "progressive sanctification." This is the life-long process of changing yourself into looking more like your Savior each day. That is what the word Christian means – little Christ. The way this is accomplished is to begin to "see" yourself in your mind's eye as God "sees" you. You are His beloved child and He wants you to develop a life-long love affair with Him and His Son. This is well worth the effort for the here and now and the here after. Every believer in the Lord Jesus Christ is worthy to receive spiritual prosperity from God.

Does God Really Love Me?

Many of the people I work with have a deep abiding love for God and His Son. Yet when I ask them if they think God loves them, they will either say He could not possibly love them, or they believe it in their heads but not in their hearts. This is the most important thing for all of us to grasp, how much He truly loves you and me! Here are but a few Scriptures that speak of God's love for us.

- "God loves me so much He sacrificed His own Son to cover my sins," (John 3:16)

- "I am His child and very precious to Him," (Romans 8:16)

- "I can do all things through Christ who strengthens me," (Philippians 4:13)

- "Greater is He that is in me than he (the devil) who is in the world," (1st John 4:4)

- "Beloved I wish that you may prosper and be in health as your soul prospers," (John 1:2)

Who Will These Counseling Techniques Benefit?

These counseling techniques, which are a gift from our loving heavenly Father, will help anyone who applies them to their lives. I urge parents to instill in their children an understanding of the "Christ-like" self-image at an early age. The sooner the child begins to realize how precious and important he is to the heavenly Father, the better his life will be. He will truly have the Fruit of the Spirit working in his life. Begin today to help your child or grandchild develops their self-talk into "God-talk" about their position in Christ and their value as a child of God.

Chapter Two

Security and Significance
- Our Basic Needs

> The truly well adjusted person is one who depends on God and what He provides to give him security (love) and significance (value). God's provisions include the church.

There are two basic needs that all people <u>must</u> have met in their lives. These are significance (purpose, value, meaningfulness) and security (unconditional love, acceptance). How these basic needs are met in our childhood will have a great impact on our self-image or self-worth.

When we are born, our parents or guardians meet our initial basic needs. As we get older, others will also begin to influence how these needs are met. This will include anyone who has close personal contact with us. This is why it is important that our parents protect us from child predators who can affect our self-image in a very negative way.

Jesus and Our Basic Needs

Before we meet Jesus as our Lord and Savior, He has zero effect on our security and significance. When we accept Him as our Savior we begin the glorious adventure of having Him become the most important contributor to our basic needs. To paraphrase Dr. Crabb in *Effective Biblical Counseling:* Every problem with our self-image can be traced directly to a wrong assumption about how to meet our basic needs for security and significance! To change our self-image we must not be concerned with changing our feelings, our behavior, or our circumstances. We must renew our mind by applying the holy Word of God. (Romans 12:1, 2)

Jesus and Our Love & Value Tank

Within each of us there is a "L&V (love & value) tank" that needs to be filled. I believe that most Christians are walking around with their L&V tank almost empty. We try to pull the needed love and value from those around us, especially our family. This puts a great deal of strain on our relationships because most people do not have any to spare.

The question I often hear from my clients is, "How do I learn to make Jesus the major source for my basic needs?" Or to state it another way, "How can I learn to let Jesus fill my L&V tank?" There are at least three things that can be done.

The first step is the most important. You must decide that the Word of God is true regardless of how things look or how you feel. This step gives you a "stake in the ground" to anchor steps two and three.

Step two is to begin to change the negative pictures in your subconscious photo album. Those pictures stop you from believing that God loves you unconditionally and considers your worth to be beyond value.

The third step is to begin to do things as an offering to your heavenly Father. You no longer expect rewards or payoffs when you do things for others. Instead you trust your Father in Heaven to meet your basic needs. When you do the act of offering to the Lord, say to yourself: "Lord I am doing this as an offering to You. I am not expecting anything back from the person I am doing it for; I am looking to You to meet my need for security and significance. This act of sacrifice does at least three things:

(1) It takes the pressure off the relationship with the person you are doing an act of service to because you are not expecting anything back from them.

(2) Based on the principle of sowing and reaping in the Bible, you are giving God something to multiply back to you to meet your basic needs.

(3) God will pour into your life a 30, 60 or 100 fold return on what you did as a true offering to Him. No matter how small or insignificant you may think the offering is; God is looking

at the attitude of your heart, not the size of the offering.

Remember, as your "love & value tank" begins to fill with the unconditional love and value that God gives you, less and less pressure will be placed on the relationships around you. In fact, God's agape love and value will overflow out of you and spill over into other lives.

Case Study

Margo came into my office looking defeated and overwhelmed by life. She was in a marriage that she described as unfulfilling. She felt unappreciated by her husband and her children. She said that no one seemed to appreciate the effort she put into having everything perfect in her home.

In reviewing her childhood, it became apparent that she had a very critical and demanding mother who only met Margo's basic needs if Margo was totally compliant and met her mother's expectations. Based on her childhood experiences, she believed her need for security and significance could only be satisfied by performing at or near perfection in everything she did. When the people around her did not recognize her efforts, then her need for feeling loved and valued was not met and the level of her L&V tank dropped even lower.

Margo had come to believe that her basic needs could only be met if she was perfect and non-confrontational in all situations. She also looked to her husband and children to meet all of her needs for love and purpose.

I explained to Margo that her husband would not be able to meet more than about ten percent of her basic needs and her children, even less. It would be necessary for her to go to Jesus Christ for most of her security and significance needs.

Margo had accepted Jesus as her Savior at ten years old, but had never given any thought to how He could meet her basic needs. I told her that Jesus would always love her unconditionally and consider her to have great worth as a child of God. His agape love for her would allow her to make mistakes and stand up for herself in a loving, Christian manner.

This was the beginning point for Margo to change her subconscious picture album. Once she realized that her basic needs could only be met through Christ, the process of instilling godly pictures in the subconscious picture album began. She realized that her drive for perfection had created problems in her marriage and with her children. Margo began to believe that the Lord Jesus would meet the majority of her basic needs. She used a personalized John 3:16 which stated, "I am loved by my Master so much that He died for me. He loves me even though I am not perfect. My worth is beyond value!"

When Margo began to rely on the Lord for the majority of her basic needs it took pressure off the husband and children to meet those needs. Everyone is much happier and the marriage is flourishing.

Chapter Three

Overcoming the Fruits of Unforgiveness: Anger and Guilt

Of the seven deadly sins, without a doubt anger is the most enjoyable. To think how someone has mistreated you is to enjoy a wonderful-tasting dish. The only drawback to this wonderful feast is that you are the main course. Anger destroys the vessel that contains it.

Often in my practice I see the results of the anger, guilt, and hostility that a person experienced as a child manifest years later. We often think of only the physical type of abuse between a parent and a child. Actually, verbal and mental abuse can be even more devastating to the self-image of the young person. This abuse may place within the child's subconscious picture album a belief that they are an "un." Which begs the question, "What is an un?" A person that is an "un" contains within their subconscious picture album many of the following: I am <u>un</u>lovable, I am <u>un</u>intelligent, I am <u>un</u>friendly, I am <u>un</u>wanted, I am <u>un</u>worthy, and on and on the "uns" go. This belief in their "uns" will convince them that they deserve to be mistreated or to mistreat others. Very often this will express itself in the marriage relationship as well as in parenting.

In addition to the damage your anger and guilt causes to others, you are the largest recipient of these destructive emotions. In the book *None of These Diseases,* fifty-one illnesses are listed that are caused primarily by anger, which is often a fruit of unforgiveness. These include high blood pressure, heart attack, colitis, and arthritis. Dr. Henry Brant stated "Approximately 97 percent of the cases of bleeding ulcers without organic origin I have dealt with were caused by anger." If you are struggling with this sin take heart because it, like all other sins, can be overcome with the help of the Holy Spirit and your willingness to work diligently with Him. As you read this book and apply it, you will begin uncovering the things in your subconscious that are causing you to react to life in a hostile and angry way.

<u>Something to think about</u>: Most anger and guilt are caused by Unforgiveness. (The one exception is righteous anger. We should not be angry when we are wronged personally, but anger when God is insulted is allowed, although even that anger should be given over to God by the time you go to bed that night.)

<u>Case Study - Anger & Guilt</u>

Sally came into my office and almost immediately broke down into a deep, racking sob. She explained that she would often lose control and fly into an uncontrollable rage. Interestingly, she pointed out that she seemed to inflict the most damage on herself in these rages and rarely, if ever, hurt anyone else. However, she was afraid that in one of these fits of anger she might hurt someone she loved, and this fear was driving her into a deep depression.

In discussing the situation with Sally, she shared that she was not sure she had ever received Jesus as her Savior. I explained to her that I am just a coach (teacher) and a cheerleader (encourager). She and the Holy Spirit working within her would do all the work for her to overcome this problem. Therefore, it would be necessary for Sally to accept the Lord Jesus as her Savior for my counseling techniques to work. She understood and agreed, so I walked the Roman road with her (this excellent salvation tool is in Appendix I) and she accepted Jesus as her Savior.

<u>Conscious and Subconscious Mind</u>

I explained to Sally that our mind is divided into two parts with about twenty percent being our conscious mind and eighty percent being the subconscious mind. The conscious mind is the part we use to make decisions such as accepting Jesus as our Savior. The subconscious mind is the part that acts as a camera or video recorder, which has been running since birth. We essentially have within our subconscious mind a giant picture album filled with all our life experiences. Everything that has happened to us throughout our life is recorded in this picture album.

Sally had been raised in a family that did not stress a relationship with Jesus as an important thing. They occasionally went to church, but it was more out of tradition than an interest in deepening their walk with the Lord. She was the youngest and had been seriously ill when young. As a result, her parents had not set many boundaries for her as a child. Sally felt that her father loved her but was never able to show her any affection. He was also very busy with his work and often neglected her. In contrast, her mother doted on her and had a tendency to overlook her fits of temper and, in fact, gave in to them. This reinforced their usefulness to Sally.

In gathering her personal data for me, she related that her brothers resented her. They had taken every opportunity to damage her self-image by referring to her as an invalid, useless, stupid, and ugly. The father took very little action to discipline the boys for this activity, thereby reinforcing in Sally's young mind that what they said must be true. Her mother was very timid and fearful of the father and did not encourage or edify Sally in any meaningful way. This further convinced Sally that her feelings of anger and inferiority were correct. Thus, more damaging pictures were placed in her subconscious photo album to be drawn on for the rest of her life unless they were changed.

Her experiences in school were also destructive to her self-image because the natural cruelty of her classmates was directed at her as one of the weakest and least secure among them. When I asked her to assess her experience in high school, her response to me was that she was a zero. She found the only time she could gain relief from the malice of her classmates, as well as her brothers, was by giving into her anger and letting it build to almost uncontrollable rage.

I also identified her basic assumptions on how she could gain security and significance. Her basic assumption was that her security rested on controlling people with her outbursts of anger.

Listening to Self-Talk

At this stage we began the work of changing her poor self-image into the "Christ-like" self-image she desired. I again explained to her that she and the Holy Spirit would begin changing the pictures in the picture album in her subconscious to reflect how God, her heavenly Father, saw her. She would be able to do this because the Holy Spirit came to live in her when she accepted Jesus as her Savior. Her assignment was to begin listening to her "self-talk" and write down on three-inch by five-inch cards everything she told herself.

I related to her that we have many ways of communicating with the subconscious. One method is when we are talking out loud to others or ourselves. Another method is the internal conversation we are continually carrying on within our mind. This is called "self-talk" and is often where the "pictures" in your subconscious will show up. This will cause you to have thoughts about yourself that do not reflect how your Father in heaven sees you.

When she brought in her cards from listening to her self-talk and they contained the following:

(1) I am angry because no one loves me;

(2) No one likes me;

(3) I am stupid;

(4) God doesn't care about me because I don't measure up;

(5) I cannot do anything right.

I explained that the next step was to try to determine where these thoughts came from originally. I told her that all children are totally egocentric. As a child and a young adult, she believed that everything that happened to her was because of something she had or had not done. For example, if her brothers tormented her, then it must be her fault. If her father did not hug her and hold her in his lap, it must be her fault, and on and on it goes. I told her it was important that she realize that the people who had placed these negative photos in her subconscious picture album were not God. They were not the pictures that her heavenly Father wanted her to have as one of His children.

The Creative Subconscious

We then discussed a mechanism within the subconscious mind That Lou Tice in his book *Smart Talk* called the "creative subconscious." The creative subconscious observes the photos in your subconscious picture album and then actively tries to project those pictures into the "real" world. In other words, the photos you have in your subconscious mind will be used by the creative subconscious to make your real world experiences match your subconscious pictures; it will try to create a "just like me" experience for your daily activities. For example, if you believe you do not deserve to be successful in business, you will unconsciously alienate your co-workers or clients and cause yourself to fail. When you commit the blunder you may even say to yourself, "Why did I do that? I knew better." Your creative subconscious has undone your best efforts again.

I asked her if she had ever met someone and had determined that she wanted to be their friend and the other person also indicated they wanted to establish a friendship. However, it seemed that although the other person stated they wanted her friendship, they did things to constantly undermine it. I told Sally what was probably happening was that although the person wanted a friend in their conscious mind (the reasoning, thinking 20 percent); in their subconscious mind (the 80 percent that contains their picture album) they probably felt they did not deserve a friend and were not worth a person spending time with them. As the creative subconscious looked at the "un" pictures, it then created situations to cause the friendship to fail. She said she had met people like that, and in fact, she felt she had done that very thing herself. She had destroyed relationships with people she really wanted to be close to but had continually done things that caused the other person to terminate the friendship. She further stated she was often furious with herself for what she had done and did not understand why she had done it until now.

Using the Cards to Correct Sally's Self-Image

I told her we would place a Scripture on each of her cards stating what God said about her. She was replacing her destructive self-talk with "God-Talk," which is what He said she was like and possessed according to His Word. In other words, whenever one of her non-edifying thoughts came into her mind she was to immediately say with all the emotion she could bring to bear "That is a lie because the Word of God says _____ about me."

NOTE: In Appendix II are several Scriptures that can be used to correct the pictures in your subconscious that do not reflect who you are as a child of God.

Card 1: Old Thought - I am angry because no one loves me unconditionally.

Sally chose for her memorization Scripture, John 3:16 - "For God so loved the world that He gave His only begotten Son, that whoever believes in Him should not perish but have everlasting life."

She then personalized it to be – God loved me so much that His Son Jesus was willing to come to earth to save me from my sins. What great value God must place on me as His daughter. My worth has been determined by God to be above any price and I will acknowledge my value in Him continually.

I told her *every time* this old thought came into her mind she was too immediately and with high emotional content repeat her personalized Scripture.

Another scripture she chose to memorize was Matt. 22:37-40; "Jesus said to him, you shall love the Lord your God with all your heart, with all your soul, and with your entire mind. This is the first and great commandment. And the second is like it: 'You shall love your neighbor as yourself.'"

She personalized that Scripture to: I will love God and Jesus with all my heart and I will love and treat others with the same love. I told her Jesus had commanded her to love herself and He would never ask her to do something she could not do and that the Holy Spirit would be helping her.

Card 2: Old Thought - No one likes me:

The verses she memorized were Ephesians 4:32 – "And be you kind one to another, tenderhearted, forgiving one another, even as God for Christ's sake has forgiven you."

Her modified Scripture was: I am kind to everyone, tenderhearted, and forgiving because God for Christ's sake forgave me.

And Proverbs 18:24 – "A man that has friends must show himself friendly: and there is a friend that sticks closer than a brother."

She personalized it to be: I have friends because I am faithful to them and sensitive to their needs and always ready to help.

Card 3: Old Thought - I am stupid:

Sally chose James 1:5, 6 – "If any of you lacks wisdom, let him ask of God, who gives to all liberally and without reproach, and it will be given to him. But let him ask in faith, with no doubting, for he who doubts is like a wave of the sea driven and tossed by the wind."

She modified it to read: If I lack wisdom, I will ask God for it and He will give it to me. I will ask in faith knowing that He will not fail me.

Card 4: Old Thought - God doesn't care about me because I don't measure up:

Sally chose: Ephesians 3:17-19 – "That Christ may dwell in your hearts by faith; that you being rooted and grounded in love, May be able to comprehend with all saints what is the breadth, and length, and depth, and height; And to know the love of Christ, which passes knowledge, that you might be filled with all the fullness of God."

She personalized it to read: Christ dwells in my heart by faith and I am rooted and grounded in His love for me. I am able to comprehend how much He loves me and I know His love for me, which passes human knowledge, and I am filled with the fullness of God.

Card 5: Old Thought - I cannot do anything right:

Sally chose Romans 8:31 – "What shall we then say to these things? If God be for us, who can be against us?"

Which she changed to: If God is for me, who can be against me!

She also chose II Peter 1:5-8 – "But also for this very reason, giving all diligence, add to your faith virtue, to virtue knowledge, to knowledge self-control, to self-control perseverance, to perseverance godliness, to godliness brotherly kindness, and to brotherly kindness love. For if these things are yours and abound, you will be neither barren nor unfruitful in the knowledge of our Lord Jesus Christ."

She personalized it to: With diligence, I will add virtue to my faith and to virtue knowledge and will gain self-control which will give me perseverance which will make me more godly and help me to be kinder and more loving. These things belong to me because I am a Child of God and Jesus is my Brother and Friend as well as my Savior.

Case Summary

Sally was highly motivated to change what was happening in her life. This counseling method is not easy and requires determination on the part of the client. I told her it would take about thirty days for the "Godly" confessions to begin altering the incorrect pictures in the subconscious picture album, so she should not get discouraged!

Sally began to review all the unforgiveness she had in her heart and as an act of her will, she began to forgive everyone she felt had hurt her. I told her it was also important to forgive herself, after she had repented and asked God for forgiveness. This was essential for addressing her issues of self-guilt. I told her that all forgiveness is not something we do when we feel like it; we do it as an act of obedience to the commands of our Lord Jesus. This is the phrase I suggested she use: "Lord Jesus, in obedience to your command, I forgive _____, I don't feel like forgiving them (or myself), but as an act of faith I forgive them to please You." I explained to her that unforgiveness damages our ability to have the Fruit of the Spirit present in our lives because it damages our fellowship with Him. *I told her that true forgiveness would be achieved not when she "forgot about it," but when the offence did not matter to her when she thought about it.*

Galatians 5:22-23; "But the fruit of the Spirit is love, joy, peace, longsuffering, kindness, goodness, faithfulness, gentleness, self-control. Against such there is no law."

Sally has made great progress and is beginning to enjoy the Fruit of the Spirit, especially self-control. She no longer is as tempted to have anger or guilt in her life for she now understands that she cannot be angry with someone if she immediately forgives them (or herself) for the trespass. In addition, she now is actively looking to Jesus for the majority of her significance and security needs and is much less demanding on those around her.

Her entire life has changed because now the creative subconscious sees the "Godly" photos in her picture album and is actively reaching out into the real world to make them come to pass. She is an example of a "Slow Motion Miracle" because she had not been able to conquer her anger and guilt until she recognized she had "pictures" to change in her subconscious. She needed the power of the Holy Spirit working with her. Once she accepted His help, the change was rapid and permanent!

Chapter Four

Overcoming Fear, Anxiety, and Worry

> Victor Hugo said, "Have courage for the great sorrows of life and patience for the small ones. And when you have finished your daily task, go to sleep in peace. God is awake!"

<u>Something to think about</u>: Fear, anxiety, and worry (with the exception of the reverential fear of God) are a direct result of not taking God at His Word regarding His interest in your life and how much He loves you.

Fear, anxiety, and worry are what I call the unholy trinity. Much of my practice involves people struggling with these three problems and the resultant devastation on their lives. Remember that I only counsel Christians because my counseling techniques rely on the Holy Spirit for change to occur. If they don't know the Lord Jesus as their Savior, the first thing I do is introduce them to Him,

31

thereby allowing the Holy Spirit to take up residence within them. What that means is that, although the people I work with are born again and have the assurance of Salvation and the promises of Scripture that God is their loving Father, they still struggle with unbelief and a lack of faith in His provisions for them.

There are basically two types of fear, according to Vine's *An Expository Dictionary of New Testament Words.* One is reverential fear, which through the indwelling Holy Spirit will serve as a controlling motive in your life in matters spiritual and moral. It is not a mere fear of His power and righteous retribution, but a wholesome dread of displeasing Him. The second fear for the Christian occurs because of lack of trust in your heavenly Father and His plans for your life. Without a strong trust in God's promises for you, there is no foundation on which to base your needs. I tell my clients that it is important to carry three percent and let God carry ninety-seven percent of the load.

A word picture I provide is a farmer at the time of Christ with a donkey and an ox. He builds a yoke for the two of them with ninety-seven percent of the power being provided by the oxen and three percent being provided by the donkey. That is a picture of Jesus and us. Of course He could easily do it all, but He wants us to work with Him to deepen our fellowship.

When the load of providing what you need falls only on your shoulders, the weight of not trusting God is too much for you to handle and the "children" of this fear raise their ugly heads: hello "worry," hello "anxiety."

What Is Fear?

Fear has been defined as the paralyzing emotion that inhibits or restricts normal feelings of love, confidence, and well being. It can trigger negative thought patterns, which can multiply like a giant snowball and consume a person's entire life. Many things can cause fear, anxiety and worry to become an issue in your life. Some of the leading causes are:

- Temperament: Many people are more prone to fear because of their temperament (For an excellent discussion on temperaments, I recommend Dr. LeHaye's book, *Why Do You Act the Way You Do*).

- Experiences you had as a child that were traumatic or frightening.

- A fear that God will not love you or provide protection for you because of some past actual or perceived sin that has occurred.

A useful Scripture to assist in overcoming fear is:

1 John 4:18; "There is no fear in love; but perfect love casts out fear, because fear involves torment. But he who fears has not been made perfect in love."

What God is saying in this marvelous Scripture is: As you understand how much He loves you, then the fear that is being forced on you by the world, the flesh, and the Devil will leave and you will have the peace that passes all understanding.

What Is Anxiety?

Many of my clients struggle with what is defined as anxiety. They have allowed their fears to drive them to "what if" scenarios. These scenarios play out as: What if I lose my job? What if my child gets ill? What if my husband gets tired of me? The "what ifs" are infinite in their variations. I explain to them that this is a favorite tool of their enemy, the devil. If he can get them to focus on "what if" then they cannot exercise faith in God's provision for them. How can they tell others how wonderful it is to be a follower of Christ and yet be consumed with concerns about the future? This state of being anxious damages or may even destroy their witness as a child of the King. The Bible gives an excellent antidote for anxiety.

Philippians 4:6,7: "Be anxious for nothing, but in everything by prayer and supplication, with thanksgiving, let your requests be made known to God; and the peace of God, which surpasses all understanding, will guard your hearts and minds through Christ Jesus."

It is important to note that anxiety has its source in the mind! This is why it is so important to revise the pictures you hold in your subconscious to reflect how much God loves you and wants you to prosper and be in health as your soul prospers.

What Is Worrying?

One definition of worrying in Webster's dictionary is "To seize by the throat with teeth and shake or mangle, as one animal does another, or to harass by repeated biting and snapping." This describes what I often hear when people begin telling me what is going on in their lives. They are being shaken and pushed around by their worries. I point out to them that the devil uses worry to defeat them with concerns that will probably never come to pass. I ask them to list all the things they have worried about in the last few weeks and then beside the listed items put a check mark by the ones that actually happened. They discover without exception that few, if any, are real issues to be concerned about.

I explain that Satan knows he cannot stop them from going to heaven. So the next best thing for him to do is to damage or destroy their testimony about the peace that should be evident in a child of God who trusts in His provision. A Scripture that I often recommend to combat worry is:

Matthew 6:25;"Therefore I say to you, do not worry about your life, what you will eat or what you will drink; nor about your body, what you will put on. Is not life more than food and the body more than clothing?

Worry simply boils down to a lack of understanding of how much God loves us and wants us to be totally trusting in His providence. Providence, unfortunately, is a word not used in the church very often today, and that is a great tragedy. What the doctrine of providence proclaims is that nothing happens to one of God's children that does not go by His throne for approval first. The book of Job clearly teaches that Satan can do nothing to one of God's own without prior approval from God. What that means is when tragedy does come into our lives; our task is to realize God is in control and wants us to grow in our relationship with Him through the situation. It is a sad fact for all of us that we grow the most in our relationship with God during the tough times.

We may praise Him and enjoy Him in times that are good, but very little real growth occurs. In the *Reformation Study Bible* there is an excellent definition of providence: "The doctrine of providence teaches Christians that they are never in the grip of blind fortune, chance, luck, or fate. All that happens to them is divinely planned, and each event comes as new summonses to trust, obey, and rejoice, knowing that all is for one's spiritual and eternal good." To sum up the providence of God, we need to understand God is sovereign and trust that He really loves us and has our best interest at heart. This is very difficult to do during the time of trial. However, it is clearly evident when we look back on the situation. If we allow the Lord to work His will in our life and not rebel, then we will move toward Him instead of away from Him.

Romans 8:28; "And we know that all things work together for good to those who love God, to those who are the called according to His purpose."

Case Study - Overcoming Fear, Worry, and Anxiety

A Christian physician that I worked closely with in the past had referred Joe to me. He would send me patients that he felt were in need of spiritual counseling in addition to their medical needs. In my opinion, spiritual issues rather than physical ones cause a large percentage of the illnesses that affect the population of the United States and probably most of the industrialized world. In fact,

Doctors tell us that 65 to 80 percent of all illnesses are emotionally induced. The Word of God says, "A merry heart does good, like medicine, But a broken spirit dries the bones." (Prov.17: 22)

Joe was on several medications for anxiety attacks, depression, and an inability to get a good night's rest. He told me he was at the "end of his rope" and was desperate to make changes in his life. After confirming that he knew the Lord Jesus as his Savior, I told him that being motivated to change was one of the key ingredients to overcoming his anxiety. I explained that the counseling techniques I use are not magic, but with his willingness to work hard and his allowing the Holy Spirit to be his partner and guide, we would both witness what I call a "Slow Motion Miracle."

During the first session I normally take a personal history to get a general idea of what types of issues clients are dealing with in their life. I also look for some of the key photos in their subconscious picture album. A pattern of desertion had started for Joe when his father left the family when he was four years old. His mother had blamed him for her husband leaving because she had gotten pregnant and had not wanted a child. Joe received no affirmation of his value as a child and was told often that he was a mistake. In addition, his experiences in school were not positive because he suffered from a learning disability that was not diagnosed until he was in high school. He was unable to established friendships, which further increased his feelings of being stupid and a social outcast.

Joe related to me that he had been married three times. He said, in each of these relationships his wife ended up treating him as his father and mother had treated him. Each marriage would last about two or three years before that person would desert him. I explained to him how a child is very egocentric, which means that they think the entire world revolves around them and their needs. Therefore, when his father deserted the family, even if his mother had not accused him of being the reason the father left, Joe would have assumed it was his fault. In accepting the responsibility for the father leaving, Joe had placed photos in his subconscious picture album. These pictures indicated that he did not deserve to be loved or cared for. As a child He believed that he must have done something to drive his father away and make his mother hate him. Joe also assumed that his inability to do well in school was totally his fault and that he did not deserve to have any friends.

I asked Joe to begin listening to his self-talk. I explained to him that self-talk is the conversation we carry on with ourselves inside our mind continuously. I asked him to begin to write down what he told himself in those internal conversations. I advised Joe to not edit what he said to himself but write it down on the three-inch by five-inch cards I provided and to include the emotion that came with the self-talk. I explained that most of his internal conversations were coming up from pictures in his subconscious and that he was not even aware they were there. I told Joe that he and the Holy Spirit would begin to changes those pictures to reflect how God saw him. The "God-Talk" he was going to begin confessing would erase the bad pictures the world, the flesh and the devil had placed in his subconscious. Those destructive pictures were no longer going to prevent him from being the man that God wanted him to be!

Joe struggled with filling out his cards and for a few sessions would "forget" them or have some other excuse for not having done them. I counseled him that this process would be painful because he would be "pulling the scab" off photos in his picture album that had not healed and were still injecting their poison into his thought life. I told Joe what he and the Holy Spirit were doing was changing his damaged self-image into the "Christ-like" self-image where he would begin to see himself as God sees him. Joe was in the process of renewing his mind.

Romans 12: 2: "And do not be conformed to this world, but be transformed by the renewing of your mind, that you may prove what is that good and acceptable and perfect will of God.

After a little more encouragement, Joe brought in the following cards:

1. I am afraid that I will never have a good marriage.

2. I have anxiety attacks when I think about my children and what may happen to them.

3. I have serious doubts about my worth as a person.

4. I am afraid that God really doesn't love me because I am such a mess.

5. I am angry with myself for worrying about things I can do nothing about.

At this point I began to help Joe understand more about the pictures in his subconscious and how his creative subconscious was reviewing those photos and projecting them into his everyday world to create an existence that looks like what his subconscious calls "just like me." The "just like me" pictures reflect how the subconscious thinks the world should treat him and will do what ever is necessary to cause the external world to match his internal pictures. Joe was beginning to have an understanding of why it was so critical to change the photos in his subconscious mind to reflect how God saw him. Joe was determined to only focus on God's pictures of how much He loved him and would protect him. This is what he would place in his subconscious picture album.

Joe told me about a relationship that he valued with a woman, and in fact he thought he might actually be in love with her. He related to me that initially their friendship had grown and she had seemed to be interested in taking it to a deeper level. He shared that he often did things that damaged their friendship without meaning to do them. In his words, "They are the opposite of what I want to do to help our relationship grow stronger, but I cannot seem to help myself." I asked him if he thought his creative subconscious might be interfering because of the photos in his picture album. Were they possibly showing him never having a fulfilling relationship with a woman? He said he would think about it and tell me the next session.

Using the Cards to Correct Joe's Self-Image

Before our next session, Joe called me and said that he thought I was right about his creative subconscious destroying his friendship with the women he had mentioned. He was excited to begin correcting his pictures. When Joe came in for the next session, we began to develop what his response would be when these damaging, destructive thoughts came into his mind.

Card One – Old Thought: I am afraid I will never have a good marriage.

Joe chose for his memorization Scripture, Philippians 4:6, 7: "Be careful for nothing; but in every thing by prayer and supplication with thanksgiving let your requests be made known unto God. And the peace of God, which passes all understanding, shall keep your hearts and minds through Christ Jesus."

He personalized it to read – I am not worried about anything because by prayer and request, with continual thanksgiving to my Father in heaven, I know he hears my prayers and He will give me peace that passes all understanding. I will keep my thoughts on my Lord Jesus and how much He loves me.

Card Two –Old Thought: I have anxiety attacks when I think about my children and what may happen to them.

Joe chose for his memorization Scripture, John 14:27 – "Peace I leave with you, my peace I give unto you: not as the world giveth, give I unto you. Let not your heart be troubled, neither let it be afraid."

He then personalized it to be — I have the peace that Jesus promised me, no matter what the world, the flesh, or the devil tell me, I know that I do not need to be afraid or troubled because Jesus told me He gives me His peace and I have it because of my faith in Him.

Card Three – Old Thought: I have serious doubts about my worth as a person.

Joe chose for his memorization Scripture, John 3:16 – "For God so loved the world that He gave His only begotten Son, that whoever believes in Him should not perish but have everlasting life."

He then personalized it to be – God loved me so much that His Son Jesus was willing to come to earth to save me from my sins. What great value God must place on me as His son. My worth has been determined by God to be above any price and I will acknowledge my value in Him continually.

Card Four –Old Thought: I am afraid that God really doesn't love me because I am such a mess.

The Scripture Joe chose was, Romans 5:8 – "But God demonstrates His own love toward us, in that while we were still sinners, Christ died for us."

His personalization was – God told me He knew I was a mess, a sinner, and yet He still demonstrated His love for me by sending His beloved Son to die in my place and give me everlasting life in His Kingdom.

Card Five – Old Thought: I am angry with myself for worrying about things I can do nothing about.

The Scripture he used to change this picture in his picture album was Matthew 6:25 - "Therefore I say to you, do not worry about your life, what you will eat or what you will drink; nor about your body, what you will put on. Is not life more than food and the body more than clothing?"

He personalized it to – Jesus tells me not to worry about my life or any of the issues surrounding it. He tells me to focus on my relationship with Him and He will take care of my needs, as I am a faithful and diligent follower of Him.

I told Joe it was important that he memorize these personalized Scriptures and every time a thought appeared in his mind that did not reflect how God saw him, he was to reject it using one of his personalized Scriptures and to do it with as much emotion as he could apply to his confession. He agreed to try doing this for one month to see how it would work in his life.

Case Summary

In one month we had began to witness a "Slow Motion Miracle" as the Word of God began to change Joe's self-image from one of worry, anxiety and fear to a self-image that reflected who he was in Jesus Christ. The "Christ-like" self-image was beginning to manifest itself in his life. I counseled him that he must still guard against the world, the flesh, and the devil trying to destroy his new self-image in Christ, but he is well on his way. By the way, his relationship with the woman he was interested in is going well.

Chapter Five

Unforgiveness and Depression

Karl Menninger, a famous psychiatrist, during a lecture on mental health was asked, "What would you advise a person to do if they felt a nervous breakdown coming on?" Most people expected him to reply, "Consult a psychiatrist." To their astonishment, he replied, "Lock up your house, go across the railroad tracks, find someone in need, and do something to help that person."

Something to Think About: I am convinced that the majority of the problems facing people today are not chemical or physical, but are spiritual. If people would only change their self-image to reflect what God says about them as a believer, most of their mental issues would resolve themselves.

I would estimate that 90 percent of the people I work with have depression as one of their primary complaints.

Why it is that depression in the United States is epidemic when we are blessed above every other nation on earth? I have heard that up to 50 percent of the population of this country is on some kind of medication to address depression or associated maladies.

Depression can be defined as undue sadness, dejection or melancholy. My clients often express feelings of worthlessness, guilt, and apprehension. As we begin to explore what creates these feelings, there is usually no external cause or one that is inappropriate. In my studies I have discovered that some personalities are characteristically mildly depressed and pessimistic. This type of personality is often called a melancholy temperament.

Melancholies often tend to develop an inadequate self-image from early childhood. This can create a lack of self-worth in their subconscious mind. If the melancholy guards his thought processes and refuses to indulge in the mental sins of anger, resentment, self-persecution, and self-pity, he is more likely not to yield to his predisposition toward depression. The melancholy person is the type who considers the glass to be half empty as opposed to half full. He also may be inclined to believe that the glass really has a slow leak. The important thing for all temperaments to remember is: *If you continually think on what the Christ-like self-image is and apply it to yourself, you will be inclined to not fall into depression!*

As you can determine from the comments above, the melancholy temperament is the one most predisposed toward depression, although all four temperaments can be affected by it. As a general rule, depression is a symptom of an underlying spiritual issue that has not been resolved. This is very often an issue of unforgiveness, either to someone else or to themselves. In fact, I find that about half the time in my counseling sessions, unforgiveness to oneself is a bigger issue than forgiving others.

In *Happiness is a Choice,* Dr. Minirth and Dr. Meier state "Most human depression is the result of our own irresponsible behavior-our own irresponsible handling of our anger and guilt. … The irresponsible action of holding grudges is what brings on the majority of depressions." They go on to state that as you hold an unconscious grudge, serotonin and norepinephrine gradually become depleted from your brain amine supplies and depression can result.

It is important to remember that all my clients are Christians and have been taught about forgiveness. Unfortunately they have rarely been taught about the importance of forgiving themselves. Once they have repented of their sin and ask for God's forgiveness, they must forgive themselves.

I ask my clients to make two lists:

<u>List one</u> is for all the things or people you need to forgive. Be specific; don't say, "I need to forgive dad." List every item you can think of and allow the Holy Spirit to take you as far back into your childhood as possible.

<u>List two</u> is for all the items you feel guilty about. For this list you must first go to God and repent (turn away from the sin) and ask Him for forgiveness. Once you

have received forgiveness from Him you must forgive yourself.

Use a confession something like this to address the unforgiveness issues in your life: "Father in obedience to your Word I forgive (someone's name or yours) because I believe Your Word and I want to experience unobstructed fellowship with You and Your Son, my Savior, Jesus. I don't feel like forgiving _____ but I do it as an act of submission to You."

I explain to the client that at first they will feel like a liar and a hypocrite because they don't really mean it. I then explain to them that obedience to the commands of God overrides any "feeling" they may have from their flesh or mind and their feelings will begin to change over time as they obey His Word.

In the New Testament the word forgive or one of its derivatives is used over 100 times and most often used when Jesus was speaking. It is obvious that He put a great deal of importance on the act of our forgiving others and ourselves.

Matthew 6:14, 15; "For if you forgive men their trespasses, your heavenly Father will also forgive you. But if you do not forgive men their trespasses, neither will your Father forgive your trespasses."

When Jesus said God would not forgive our trespasses, He was not saying we would lose our Salvation, which is granted by grace and not by works. However, He was stating that our lack of forgiveness would cause God to discipline us for disobedience to His Word. This discipline often takes the form of us losing our fellowship with Him. In other words, we no longer have a line of communication with Him that is "static free" and it is difficult for us to heed His leading. In addition, He may withdraw some of His protection from around us to "get our attention." God will chasten His children to help them regain their fellowship with Him.

Hebrews 12:5 - 8; "And you have forgotten the exhortation which speaks to you as to sons: "My son, do not despise the chastening of the Lord, Nor be discouraged when you are rebuked by Him; For whom the Lord loves He chastens, And scourges every son whom He receives. If you endure chastening, God deals with you as with sons; for what son is there whom a father does not chasten? But if you are without chastening, of which all have become partakers, then you are illegitimate and not sons."

I point out to my clients that forgiveness is not a suggestion by God in His Word, but is a command. When they tell me they are waiting to forgive until they "feel" like it, I tell them they are in disobedience to the Word of God. We are commanded to forgive regardless of what our feelings are on the issue or how badly we have been wronged. I share with them the story in Matthew 18:23-33.

In this parable the Lord tells us about a servant that was forgiven a debt that was so large that it was impossible for the servant to pay it. The servant then turned around and would not forgive the debt of a fellow servant who owed him very little in comparison to the debt he had received forgiveness for. When the Lord heard of the first

49

servant's actions, He called the first servant in and said, "You wicked servant! I forgave you all that debt because you begged me; should you not also have had compassion on your fellow servant, just as I had pity on you?"

It is clear from Jesus' story that we, as believers in Him, have been forgiven an insurmountable debt (our sins), therefore, God expects us to forgive others the insignificant amount they owe us. The person may feel the debt someone owes them is huge, but when compared to the debt God forgave it is always insignificant. We are to forgive every time it becomes necessary and not just "when we feel like it." The lack of forgiveness we have toward others and toward ourselves is nothing but spiritual pride and rebellion against the clear teachings of our heavenly Father. I explain to the client that unforgiveness actually gives the person you will not forgive control over your life. It can cause your spiritual life to be much less productive for the Kingdom.

<u>Something to think about</u>: If a person can knowingly commit a sin and not experience the conviction of the Holy Spirit for committing the sin (feels like guilt), they may not have truly accepted Christ Jesus as their Lord and Savior!

Case Study - Overcoming Depression and Unforgiveness

Betty came into my office looking drawn and very thin in her expensive dress and matching shoes. A secular psychologist who felt her problems extended beyond his expertise and went into the spiritual realm had recommended her to me. In talking to her during the preliminary interview it became apparent that the psychologist was correct in assessing much if not most of her problems were spiritual in nature. She was near a total nervous breakdown over her self-hatred.

As we talked, she told me that this was her second marriage and she had been married for eight years to a successful builder. Their marriage was good. Her previous marriage had been while she was still in high school due to an unplanned pregnancy. The young man she had married was from a dysfunctional family, and the father had been abusive to him and his mother, so he had brought that tradition into their young marriage as well. In addition, Betty's family was broken and her father had deserted them when she was eight. Her mother had tried to do a good job, but was so busy trying to keep food on the table for Betty and her two younger brothers that she had little time for her children.

As we continued to talk, she related to me that she had accepted the Lord Jesus in her life at eight years of age, and she had attended church on a regular basis most of her adult life. She stated, however, that she had a hard time believing that God could love her, considering what she had done. When I ask her what she had done that was so awful, she began to have a full-blown anxiety attack and was having trouble breathing. I told her to skip that matter for now and we would visit it at a later date. Other issues we talked about were how her first husband had abused her and the children. When they divorced he had taken the children with him because she was not able to provide for them. She also shared that some of the men friends her mother had brought home for an evening had sexually molested her. When she told her mother, she had not believed her. It was apparent that Betty had many photos in her subconscious picture album that we would need to address. I explained to her about how, as a child, she would incorrectly assume everything that happened to her was her fault and how this would all be stored in her subconscious mind for recall later.

A few of her pictures were:

1. Her father had deserted them and it was her fault;

2. She deserved to be physically and sexually abused;

3. She was a bad mother and had deserted her children.

In reviewing her conversation with me, it appeared that she believed to have her security and significance needs met she must be perfect and allowed others to abuse her.

In our next session I explained to her about her creative subconscious and how it would try to project the photos in her subconscious mind into the real world to make the external world to be "just like me." I asked her to use the 3-inch by 5-inch cards I provided to write down her self-talk, which was the internal conversation that she carried on inside her head. She agreed to "try it" and I told her it was imperative that she do this exercise to determine what pictures were coming up from her subconscious. I also told her to expect the process to be somewhat painful because she and the Holy Spirit would be bringing things to her remembrance that she may have buried away from her conscious memory.

The next session, she brought in several cards that read as follows:

1. It is impossible for God to love me - I am too bad.

2. My family and others mistreat me.

3. I am a cold fish and unable to respond to my husband's love.

4. I deserve to be abandoned.

5. I am foolish and make too many dumb mistakes.

6. I am a bad mother.

Betty then began slowly to tell me why she had the anxiety attack during the last session. She related that early in her marriage she had resented her first child, which was a girl. In fact, she said she had actually abused the baby and had not taken good care of it. Then when her first husband took the children after the divorce, she never had a chance to make up the bad treatment before the child had died in a fire. She told me that it would be impossible for God to forgive her and, even if He did, she could not forgive herself. This poor woman was consumed with self-hated and unforgiveness.

I gently began to discuss with her about forgiveness and asked if she had forgiven her first husband and the men who had sexually molested her. She assured me that she had carefully and consciously forgiven all that had wronged her as the Word of God commanded. I told her what she had done was commendable, but she had missed one person who needed forgiveness and that was herself. She told me that she knew God would forgive her but she could never forgive herself. I pointed out to her that her unwillingness to forgive herself after God had forgiven her was an act of spiritual pride. Basically she was saying that God's forgiveness was not sufficient to allow her to forgive herself. This statement took her completely by surprise, and after thinking about it for a few moments, she looked at me and said "You are absolutely right; I have been setting myself ahead of God in this matter."

Using the Cards to Change Betty's Self-Image

When Betty came in for the next session, I could hardly believe it was the same woman. She was laughing and much more relaxed. I ask her what had happened, and she told me she had a long talk with God. She had told Him she was accepting His forgiveness for her being a poor mother. She now recognized all her sins, including abusing her child, were covered by the Blood of Jesus. She said she was ready to begin working on the other issues in her life. So we started on the cards and the "God-Talk" she would begin using to change her subconscious pictures.

Card One – Old Thought: It is impossible for God to love me - I am too bad.

The Scripture Betty chose was: Romans 8:38, 39 – "For I am persuaded that neither death, nor life, nor angels, nor principalities, nor powers, nor things present, nor things to come, nor height, nor depth, nor any other creature, shall be able to separate us from the love of God, which is in Christ Jesus our Lord."

She personalized it to say: I am convinced that nothing can separate me from God's love because I have accepted Jesus Christ as my Savior.

Card Two – Old Thought: my family and others mistreat me.

The Scripture she chose was: II Corinthians 4:8, 9 – "We are troubled on every side, yet not distressed; we are perplexed, but not in despair; Persecuted, but not forsaken; cast down, but not destroyed;"

She personalized it to say: I may have trouble on every side, but because I know that God loves me, I am not distressed or worried about it. My significance and security are in my relationship with Jesus, my friend, elder brother and Savior.

Card Three – Old Thought: I am a cold fish and unable to respond to my husband's love.

The first Scripture she chose was; Proverbs 3:5, 6 – "Trust in the Lord with all your heart; and lean not unto your own understanding. In all your ways acknowledge Him, and He shall direct your paths."

Her personalized scripture was: I will trust Jesus with all my heart and will not try to reason everything out, but will trust in His love for me. He will help me develop a desire for my husband's love.

The second Scripture she chose was; Song of Solomon 7:1 – 10; How beautiful are your feet in sandals, O prince's daughter! The curves of your thighs are like jewels, the work of the hands of a skillful workman. Your navel is a rounded goblet; It lacks no blended beverage. Your waist is a heap of wheat Set about with lilies. Your two breasts are like two fawns, Twins of a gazelle. … A king is held captive by your tresses. How fair and how pleasant you are, O love, with your delights! This stature of yours is like a palm tree, And your breasts like its clusters. … I am my beloved's, and his desire is toward me."

She personalized this to say: God will help me develop a desire for my husband like the desire of the woman in the Song of Solomon. It is good and pleasing to God that the marriage bed be a place of fulfillment for men and women's sexual needs. There is nothing wrong with sex within marriage, and it will be a wonderful experience for my husband and me. It is a way of expressing my love and admiration for him.

Card Four – Old Thought: I deserve to be abandoned.

Betty's first Scripture was; John 14:27 – "Peace I leave with you, my peace I give unto you; not as the world gives, give I unto you. Let not your heart be troubled, neither let it be afraid."

She personalized it to read: I have the peace of Christ, which passes all understanding. I am His child and deserve to be treated as one. I will never be abandoned again because my Lord and my God is always with me.

Her second Scripture was; II Timothy 1:7 – "For God has not given us the spirit of fear; but of power, and of love, and of a sound mind."

Her personalization was: I no longer have a spirit of fear, which is from the devil, but I have a spirit of power, love and a sound mind. I no longer am afraid of being abandoned because Jesus is always with me.

Card Five – Old Thought: I am foolish and make too many dumb mistakes.

The first Scripture was; James 1:5, 6 – "If any of you lack wisdom, let him ask of God that giveth to all men liberally, and upbraideth not; and it shall be given him. But let him ask in faith, nothing wavering. For he that wavers is like a wave of the sea driven with the wind and tossed."

Her personalization was: I have the wisdom of God because I ask for it and He gives it to me. I ask in faith knowing that He wants me to succeed as His child.

Her second Scripture was; II Timothy 2:15 – "Study to show yourself approved unto God, a workman that needs not to be ashamed, rightly dividing the word of truth."

Her personalization read: I will study the holy Word of God to have the ability to rightly divide His word. This will help me know when my enemies, the world, the flesh, and the devil are trying to mislead me. I will only follow what the Word teaches.

Card Six – Old Card: I am a bad mother.

She chose; Mark 11:25 – "And whenever you stand praying, if you have anything against anyone, forgive him that your Father in heaven may also forgive you your trespasses.

Her personalization read: As I pray to the Father for forgiveness, I know I receive it because He has promised forgiveness to me in His Word. I will learn to forgive myself as I forgive all others in obedience to His command.

The second Scripture she chose was; John 16:33 – "These things I have spoken unto you, that in me you might have peace. In the world you shall have tribulation but be of good cheer; I have overcome the world."

She personalized it to say: I have peace within myself even if the world places tribulation upon me. I will no longer beat myself up for things that God has forgiven me for. I am a world overcomer!

I counseled Betty that it was critical that she commit to memory the verses she had personalized. Every time a negative thought crept into her mind, she was too forcefully and out loud, if possible, repeat her Scripture until the ungodly thought was drowned out. I told her as she continued to do this; the pictures in her subconscious would begin to change. The creative subconscious would begin to make her external world look like the new pictures. This would bring blessings to her life. I also explained that this transition would take some time. But, she should be seeing amazing results within thirty days from the day she began to make the positive confessions.

Case Summary

Now when I look at Betty when she comes into the office for her session, I am amazed at the change that has occurred in her outlook on life. She is happy and fulfilled. The sexual relationship with her husband has improved, but she says it is not yet where she wants it to be. She is active in her church and is truly becoming the woman of God that He wants her to be. She knows that it will be a life-long struggle to defeat the enemies of her soul. However, she is now equipped to do battle with the negative pictures in her subconscious. Betty is another "Slow Motion Miracle" in progress. *To God Be the Glory*!

Chapter Six

Marriage: The Church vs. The World

In the middle of a heated argument between a parson and his wife, she went to his desk and grabbed two sheets of paper and said to her husband, "Let's make a list of everything we don't like about each other." He started writing and she stared at him for a few minutes and then wrote something on her paper. Every time he stopped, she would write something down. They finally finished and gave each other their lists. "Give mine back," he asked, for all she had written on her sheet was: "I love you, I love you, I love you."

Marriage and the family were the first institution established by God. Jesus discussed it in the book of Matthew.

MT 19:4 – 6: And He answered and said to them, "Have you not read that He who made them at the beginning 'made them male and female," and said, "For this reason a man shall leave his father and mother and be joined to his wife, and the two shall become one flesh? So then, they are no longer two but one flesh. Therefore what God has joined together, let not man separate."

He was clearly stating that His Church (the people who have truly accepted Jesus as their Lord and Savior) should look differently than the world with regard to marriage. The family that is Christ centered should not look like the world's families. But the statistics for divorce in the Church and in the world look almost identical!

There was a time when people stayed together "for the sake of the children." or because they understood that two marriage ceremonies occur during the wedding. One is a civil marriage and the other is a covenant marriage between you and God. The civil contract can be broken at will but the covenant with God is much more difficult to dissolve. This is why Jesus in Matthew 5:22 said the woman who was divorce committed adultery when she remarried except for sexual unfaithfulness by the other partner. Paul expanded divorce to include desertion by an unbeliever. Remarrying for any reason besides adultery or desertion is not the unpardonable sin, but the consequences for this act will be far reaching. The people who will suffer the most are your children. In surveys, divorce ranks as a major trauma in a child's life, no matter how old they are when it occurs.

I am often asked what about an abusive situation? My counsel is that the abused person should leave the relationship and can obtain a civil divorce. However, I find no Scripture to support a covenant divorce except as listed above. Remember divorce is not the unpardonable sin, but in the long run you will be much happier to let God and His rule book, the Bible, dictate your actions.

I believe that the high incident of divorce in the church accounts for why many of our children do not understand that the Word of God is absolute authority and Jesus wasn't just a good man; He is the second part of the Trinity and is God the Son. What has gone wrong with our understanding of what the Bible so clearly teaches about marriage and the family?

Much of it has to do with our understanding of how we can achieve our security and significance. Significance is defined as that which describes who I am and why I have value as a person. Security is best defined as love that expresses acceptance for me, warts and all, or agape love.

What Is On Your Altar?

There is within us all an altar. We place on that altar what we count on to provide us with security and significance. In my marriage counseling sessions I often find that the woman has placed her husband on the altar of her heart. No man is built to occupy that position. What happens over time is he will begin to lean and eventually topple over. This occurs because none of us are built to provide total security and significance to another. That honor belongs to and can only be fulfilled by the Lord Jesus Christ.

When the man topples over, it will look like many things such as an affair, drinking, desertion, verbally abusive behavior, and the list goes on. He will feel that he has failed his wife and she will agree with him. Her world is shattered because her significance and security are gone. His world is shattered because he failed at something he never had a chance of accomplishing.

As I said earlier, only one person is able to meet the task of providing your complete need for security and significance. He is the Lord Jesus Christ. So how do you go about making Him the person you look to for these needs to be met?

Learning To Lean On Jesus

The task is to begin placing Jesus on the altar of your heart. Instead of having the Lord on your altar, many other things may be placed there. For men it may be their job, their position in the community, etc. For women it is most often their husband, their children, their beauty or it can be their house or bank account. The point I am making is if you are leaning on any of the things above for your significance and security, they will fail you at some point in your life! When that happens you will topple over and it may be very difficult to get back up. You will not lose your salvation, but you may do great harm to yourself as a witness to an unbelieving world.

The world, the flesh, and the devil have done a good job of convincing even the believing Church that riches and power are the way to secure lasting significance and security. You hear people say, "If I only had more money, or if my husband/wife would pay more attention to me, or if I had a better job and so on, I would feel secure and significant." The problem with all those things is they are temporal, which means they are of this world and not permanent. Only one person is eternal and that is Jesus.

You need to begin reviewing your self-talk. Any time you hear yourself stating that anything besides Jesus will give you the significance and security you desire, you should change that self-talk to say my entire security and significance is centered on my relationship with Jesus. Anything that provides you more security and significance than your relationship with Jesus is an idol. Never again let anything but Him occupy the altar of your heart.

Love Versus Respect and Trust

An area that often comes up in counseling couples is the issue of love versus respect and trust. Women are often astounded when they find out how important respect and trust are to their husband. In a large survey two statements were made and the participants were to say which one would be the worst for them. Statement one was "The worst thing that could happen to me is to not be loved." Statement two was "The worst thing that could happen to me is to not be respected and trusted."

Over ninety percent of the women said that statement one about not being loved was the worst. However, over ninety percent of the men said that not being respected and trusted was the worst.

When a woman feels unloved she will normally cry but when a man feels disrespected he will normally get angry or disengage from the discussion with his wife. A wise woman will observe when discussing things with her husband. If he gets angry or "shuts down" she may have accidentally disrespected him. She needs to look for opportunities to tell him she is proud of him.

It is important that a man receive advice from his wife for God has provided her as a helpmate and advisor. However, she needs to learn to disagree or advise in a way that does not make him feel disrespected. An excellent resource for learning more about this issue is *For Women Only* by Shaunti Feldhahn.

Ephesians 5:33 Nevertheless let each one of you in particular so love his own wife as himself, and let the wife see that she respects her husband

Case Study- Jesus as Your Source

I heard angry words being exchanged from outside my office and in walked John and Mary from my church. They were having what we call in the Church an "intense devotional" which is another way of describing a knockdown, drag-out argument. After a few moments they began to calm down and asked me to help them to "untangle the mess" their marriage had turned into. They are both believers in Christ and active members of the church, so I was a little surprised at the difficulty their marriage was in.

In counseling situations I normally do up to five sessions individually and then up to five together. They agreed that was acceptable to them so I started with John first. He related to me that he was no longer able to meet all of Mary's emotional needs. I asked him to explain and he stated, "She leans on me for her total emotional support. Anytime I say a word of criticism or don't like something she does, she falls apart. I am to the point where I don't know what to do." In discussing John's parents, it turned out that he had a very overbearing, critical father and these pictures had been placed in his subconscious photo album.

I next had a counseling session with Mary, and she was beside herself with anxiety and worry over her marriage to John. She said, "I love him, but sometimes I cannot stand to be around him. I am so afraid and worried that he may leave me. I know I cling to him too much, but I cannot seem to help myself." In reviewing Mary's childhood it turned out that her father had deserted them when she was eight years old.

I had each of them begin an intense review of their subconscious picture album to uncover what in there did not reflect the way God "sees" them. John began to realize that his photo album contained many pictures about his Dad's critical spirit and his lack of praise for anyone. He began to confess that he was becoming the husband that Paul described in Ephesians.

Ephesians 5:25; "Husbands, love your wives, just as Christ also loved the church and gave Himself for her."

Mary, in reviewing her subconscious picture album, realized that she had many pictures relating to desertion and abandonment. She began to understand she was projecting this fear and anxiety into her relationship with John. She found and began to apply II Timothy to her picture album to change the negative pictures contained there.

2Timothy 1:7; "For God has not given us a spirit of fear, but of power and of love and of a sound mind."

I then began to explain to them about how our security and significance must be centered on Jesus. That will keep us from toppling over and pulling everyone that is leaning on us down at the same time. Both John and Mary admitted that they had allowed people (John in Mary's case) or things (his job in John's case) to remove Jesus from the altar of their hearts. This had caused both of them to become fearful and strike out at each other. They committed to putting the Lord back where He belonged. They also affirmed they would be sure and keep Him there. Any time one of them had a thought about their significance or security being centered anywhere but Jesus, they would immediately correct it. They would forcefully state, "I am fully committed to Jesus being my source for all things."

Case Summary

John and Mary are much happier now. They can enjoy each other because most of the pressure has left their marriage. They now consider the love and affection they give each other to be in addition to what the Lord provides instead of in place of it. John has learned to be more affirming and Mary has done a great job of placing Jesus on the altar of her heart. They are now jointly teaching the young married class with great success.

Chapter Seven

Abusive Relationships

> Something to think about: Abuse of all kinds is epidemic in our world, from treating the checkout person at Wal-Mart badly to road rage. The devil is having a field day with our treatment of each other, even in the Church. The only answer for this abuse is to fill our hearts with the love of God. Then allow it to flow from us to our fellow man.

Battered and Abused Spouse

This is my most difficult chapter to write because it involves heavily co-dependent relationships. A co-dependent relationship consists of two people who, due to childhood trauma, neglect, abuse, or other factors have not developed a fully formed personality. These people need another person to complete them and often chose someone who will mistreat them both physically and mentally. Men commit most but not all spousal abuse.

The statistics demonstrate that a woman will be severely beaten an average of seven times before seeking help or shelter for herself and her children. If you are in this situation, let me encourage you to seek help the first time there is serious domestic violence in your home. Your spouse will promise to never do it again and will be very repentant, but it will only get worse without intervention. The best chance of saving your marriage and even, perhaps, your life is to get help early.

If you find yourself already in this situation, seek help from your local women's shelter. In addition, find a godly Christian counselor to help you change your "need" for an abusive relationship.

Why Do I Choose Someone Who Will Abuse Me?

The reasons a person enters into or stays in an abusive relationship are often buried in their subconscious from childhood. Many times women in this type of relationship have experienced physical, mental, or sexual abuse or perhaps all three when they were younger. Since a child is totally egocentric, they think that everything that happens is due to them. In other words, due to their egocentricity, they think that the abuse that occurs to them is their fault. This causes photos to be placed in their subconscious picture album that indicates this is how their life is going to look when they are adults. Then the creative subconscious looks at the pictures it contains and will find someone that will match the photos that say, "I deserve to be abused."

An example of this is when a woman finds herself married to a man who abuses her just like her father did. This occurs even after the person may have proclaimed to themselves and anyone that will listen, "I will never marry anyone that acts like Dad did when I was growing up."

Why Am I Codependent?

Codependents are individuals who often feel responsible for everyone's life but their own. They are the ones who seek to make everyone happy, control everyone's life, take on other's responsibilities, and the story goes on and on. The condition of codependency is primarily the result of a dysfunctional home from early childhood. What is the dysfunctional home? That is a home that does not provide the basic essentials needed to grow emotionally mature adults. The essentials needed for such growth are love, communication, acceptance, affirmation, positive self-concepts, honesty and understanding.

The person in a codependent relationship needs to learn to get her security and significance, which are two basic needs of all of us, from a relationship with Jesus Christ. It is not possible for any other person to completely fulfill those needs. Only Jesus will never let you down. It is wonderful to have a group of people who affirm you and give you love. But only Jesus can truly meet your need for security and significance. To be a mentally healthy person requires a sense of personal worth that can only be met by understanding our significance and security as being centered in Christ. This Christian self-love can only be accomplished as we understand and believe how much

God loves and approves of us. Significance is defined as that which describes who I am and why I have value as a person. Security is best defined as love that expresses acceptance for me, warts and all, or agape love.

Agape love is the unconditional love that God has for those who are His children. Interestingly, men have a tendency to rely more on significance and women rely more on security, although both are required.

Case Study - Overcoming Spousal Abuse

As Sue came into the office, I noticed she was limping and one of her wrists had a brace on it. She had been recommended to me for counseling by the women's shelter that was her current home. She was very defensive and seemed to resent the fact that she had been sent to me for counseling. As we talked, I told her I was on her side and only wanted the best for her and her two children. I also explained to her that unless she was willing to work hard and allow the Holy Spirit to help her, there was really nothing I could do for her. She began to relax and said she realized that her life could not continue as it was going. I confirmed that she knew the lord Jesus as her Savior and explained to her how the Holy Spirit and she were going to change the photos in her subconscious picture album to pictures of how her heavenly Father saw her.

She told me this was the third time for her to leave her own home and seek shelter from her second husband's violent and physically abusive behavior. She said when she met her current husband she had just received a divorce from a man who was also abusive both physically and mentally. She had married the first husband at fifteen years of age just to escape her home environment. They had two children during the fifteen years they were married.

She had sworn to herself to never marry another man like that, but she had done it again. She said their courtship had only lasted six months. During that time her second husband had been a true gentleman, opening doors for her and being very attentive. He had also been married before and said his wife had run off with another man. She said, "I learned after we were married that she had left him and moved out of state to escape his abuse and harassment." I explained to her that this was typical behavior for an abuser. While they are in the "hunting" mode they will appear to be everything a woman could want in a man. They will be attentive and supportive in every way until they capture their "target." It is really important to know the prospective new husband and his friends for at least a year. After that time an engagement for one more year is important to know even more about who you are marrying. The abuser can rarely maintain his false identity for that length of time. It is also important to talk with his friends about who he is and how he treats people.

She then began to tell me about her childhood, and we began to figure out some of the pictures that her subconscious mind contained that were causing her to repeatedly marry men who would abuse her. She told me that her mother was mentally unstable and would drift in and out of the life of the family. She said she loved her father, but he often got drunk. When he got drunk he would beat her and her two brothers until he passed out. In addition, her two brothers, who were older than her, often sexually abused her and then told her they would beat her up if she told anyone. She once did tell her mother, but she did not believe her.

It was apparent from her childhood experiences that Sue contained pictures in her subconscious that indicated she deserved to be abused. This was essentially the only form of attention she received from her dad or anyone of importance in her young life. She had concluded that she must be of no value except when she was being physically, mentally or sexually abused. These beliefs were not held in her conscious mind but they were held in her subconscious. An interesting thing about human beings is that negative attention is preferable to no attention at all.

We talked about significance and security and how those terms need to be centered on Jesus to keep us from being disappointed in people. I told her there is only one person who will never let you down and that is the Lord. Other people will not mean to fail you, but being human, sooner or later they will. She was then given 3-inch by five-inch cards. They were to be used to record her self-talk and to bring them in for the next session.

Sue brought in her cards the next session, and they were as follows:

1. I am worthless;

2. I am stupid and make bad decisions;

3. I don't believe that God really loves me;

4. I will never succeed at anything I try;

5. My life is hopeless.

As we talked about her cards, I began to show her how experiences as a child had formed the photos in her subconscious picture album. When her father would not give her any attention unless he was drinking and abusing her, it caused her to form pictures that showed that she would get attention in abusive situations only. She was totally opposed to this idea in the conscious, reasoning part of her mind, but her subconscious mind was in full agreement with this belief. Therefore, her subconscious mind would cause her to be attracted to men who would abuse her. This would insure that she would receive attention like she had received as a child. What she and the Holy Spirit were now going to do was begin changing the subconscious pictures one at a time. Replacing them with what the Word of God says about her as one of His children. She was going to begin using "God-Talk" as her new self-talk.

Using the Cards to Change Sue's Self-Image

Card One – Old Idea: I am worthless.

She chose for her Scripture; I John 3:1 – "Behold, what manner of love the Father hath bestowed upon us, that we should be called the sons of God: therefore, the world knows us not, because it knew Him not."

Mary personalized it to read: Look how much my heavenly Father loves me; I am called a daughter of God. I am of great value to Him. It does not matter what the world says about me, God says I am worthy of His love.

Card Two - I am stupid and make bad decisions.

Mary chose for her memorization Scriptures; Philippines 4:13 – "I can do all things through Christ which strengthens me." And Philippians 1:6 – "Being confident of this very thing, that He which hath begun a good work in you will perform it until the day of Jesus Christ."

She personalized it to read: I can do anything because Christ is my strength, He has begun a good work in me and He will continue doing it all the days of my life.

Card Three – Old Idea: I don't believe that God really loves me.

She chose for her Scripture; John 3:16 - "For God so loved the world that He gave His only begotten Son, that whoever believes in Him should not perish but have everlasting life."

She then personalized it to be – God loves me so much that His Son Jesus was willing to come to earth to save me from my sins. What great value God must place on me as His daughter. My worth has been determined by God to be above any price and I will acknowledge my value in Him continually.

Card Four – Old Idea: I will never succeed at anything I try.

The Scripture chosen was; James 1:5, 6 – "If any of you lacks wisdom, let him ask of God, who gives to all liberally and without reproach, and it will be given to him. But let him ask in faith, nothing wavering. For he that wavers is like a wave of the sea driven with the wind and tossed."

Her personalization was: I will succeed at everything I set my hand to because I have the wisdom of God because I ask for it and He gives it to me. I ask in faith knowing that He wants me to succeed as His child.

Card Five – Old Idea: My life is hopeless.

The Scriptures Mary chose were; II Corinthians 2:14 – "Now thanks be unto God, which always causes us to triumph in Christ, and makes manifest the savor of his knowledge by us in every place." And I John 5:4 – "For whatsoever is born of God overcomes the world: and this is the victory that overcomes the world, even our faith."

She personalized it to read: My life is full of hope because God causes me to triumph in Christ and no matter what the world, the flesh, or the devil throws at me. I know I have the victory in Jesus my friend, my elder brother and my Savior.

I told Sue this was a great start in her beginning to assume her rightful place in this world as a child of the King of the universe. I encouraged her to commit the cards to memory and any time a negative thought crept into her mind, she was to forcefully state what her position in Christ is and why she has great value as a joint heir with Christ.

Case Summary

Sue and her children are doing much better. I had counseling sessions with the children to talk with them about developing their "Christ-like" self-image. This helped them undo any lingering pictures in their subconscious mind that may create problems for them as they grow into adults. The husband was not willing to get counseling, so Sue has separated from him and has established a new and safe environment for her and her children. The police have worked with Sue to convince the husband to leave them alone. They stated they would place him in jail if he does not comply with the judge's order to stay away from her. She still has a long way to go, but the distance Sue has come so far is a "Slow Motion Miracle."

Chapter Eight

Grief Counseling

> C. S. Lewis observed, "Suffering is not good in itself. What is good in any painful experience is, for the sufferer, his submission to the will of God, and for the spectators, the compassion aroused and the acts of mercy to which it leads."

A task that we all will face from time to time is helping someone struggle through the grieving process. The most important thing you can do for the bereaved is to *listen*. Many people are not comfortable with someone grieving; they would prefer that the grieving person not talk about the loss they experienced.

Whenever a significant loss or reversal is experienced people will go through five stages of grieving. These stages can overlap each other from time to time. Grief reactions are not clinical depression but can become one if the person does not resolve stages two and three using the techniques listed in chapter five under forgiveness and guilt.

Stage one is denial and the individual refuses to believe what is happening. This stage usually does not last very long.

Stage two is one we all experience when a significant loss occurs. You will feel angry toward someone other than yourself. This may even include the person who died or left. This anger can even be felt toward God for allowing it to happen. This is a normal reaction. If you linger in this stage to long without expressing forgiveness then clinical depression can result.

Stage three is guilt, which is often a combination of false and true guilt. Remember God wants us to forgive others and ourselves for our own good. If you do not resolve the guilt it will manifest itself in depression.

Stage four is genuine grieving, which is the most important and vital stage to go through. It is important for both men and women to have a good cry. If Jesus could weep over sad situations, then we should also.

Stage five is a rather brief stage, which occurs once a person has worked through the other four stages. During this stage you will begin regaining your joy and zest for life.

When I am counseling someone who is grieving I encourage them to talk about the person, bring pictures and letters, anything that will help them come to closure with the death.

<u>Something to consider:</u> Although you may be tempted, never tell the person who is grieving to "get over it." Everyone grieves at his own speed and he will complete the process when he completes it. What you, as the counselor, need to do is stay available to the grieving person for as long as he needs you. This is not a short time commitment of your resources unless you can recruit others to offer a listening and compassionate ear.

There are several tasks for the grieving person to accomplish: (1) Help them identify secondary losses, such as plans that included the person, and any unfinished business. (2) Help them recognize that, in addition to grieving for the lost person, grief will need to be experienced for any dreams or expectations they had for the person. (3) Discover where they may be lacking in their coping skills. (4) Help them understand the potential duration and process of grieving. They should not compare their experience with anyone else's; they are unique. (5) Encourage them to go through the pain of grief. (6) Help them understand the process of grief. Help them plan for significant dates and holidays in advance. (7) Help them to find ways to replenish spiritually, socially and physically. Alert them to the potential of diminished capacity of their immune system during the grieving process. (8) Avoid all major decisions for the first year after a loss, if possible.

It is also important to remember that we grieve over many things: Loss of a job, moving from a loved home, child going to college, etc. It is important to let the person grieve, but not let them become morbid about the loss.

<u>Case Study - Grief and Morning</u>

Lee came into my office looking very tired. She had dark circles under her eyes and she had obviously been crying. As we began to talk, she began to tell me of the heartache that was tearing her life apart.

A few years earlier her grandfather had been murdered in a botched robbery attempt. He had been walking down the street and saw a woman being robbed and had tried to help her. In the process he had been fatally wounded.

Lee had never been close to her mother and her father had deserted them when she was two years old. Her grandfather was the only one who had truly loved and cared for her. She had received almost all her significance and security from their relationship.

Lee had received the Lord Jesus as her Savior when she was eight years old and had always felt close to Him until the death of her grandfather. When her grandfather was murdered she told me she "turned her back" on God. This had been going on for about five years and she was desperate to get her life back together.

I explained that her grieving experience was one of the most difficult to complete due to the violent and unexpected nature of her grandfather's death. I also told her that being angry with God is a fairly common thing for people that are grieving. Where her life had gone wrong was in staying "mad" at God for such a long period of time.

I ask her to visualize God standing beside her with His arms wide open asking her to come to Him for comfort and peace in the middle of the pain in her life. I told her that our Lord Jesus is familiar with our pain and suffering and wants to help us through the time of grieving. What she had done was move away from God instead of toward Him. This had only allowed the pain and suffering to linger instead of being healed by the Masters touch.

In our next session she brought in letters and pictures of her grandfather and we talked about him and celebrated his life and how important he was to her. We also discussed ways for her to begin obtaining a significant portion of her significance and security from her relationship with Jesus Christ.

Case Summary

Lee is doing much better now. Her nightmares about death and being murdered have completely stopped. She is growing more confident each day in her relationship with Jesus and is looking to Him for the majority of her significance and security. She understands now that "It is not a good idea to box with God because His arms are too long."

Chapter Nine

Raising Godly Kids in an Ungodly World

A major challenged facing the parent today is how to train children to serve God and their fellow man in a world where everything and everyone tells them, "it is all about me!" We are all born with a sin nature that leads us to see ourselves as the most important person, but with the child it is magnified. They are totally egocentric, they truly believe in the core of their being that the world revolves around them.

This egocentricity is the major reason that the experiences that go into the child's subconscious picture album are so important. If they are surrounded by people that teach them the importance of serving God and their fellow man, they will develop a Christian world view that will serve them well through out their life. However, if they are surrounded by people that focus mainly on themselves, they will develop a world view that everything is about me, myself and I.

How we perceive the world is called our "world view." Our world view is the filter that every decision we make passes through. If we have a Christian world view, then all our decisions are compared to the Word of God. God's word is considered absolute truth and anything that violates His clear teaching is considered unacceptable. Unfortunately, only about nine percent of evangelical Christians currently have a "Christian world view." For more on this subject I strongly recommend Focus on the Family's Truth Project teachings with Dr. Del Tacket.

Four Keys to Raising a Godly Child

I tell parents that there are four key things that they need to do to help their children develop a Christian world view.

First Key - Model Christ Jesus in your own life: Let her observe how you look to Jesus for guidance in the decisions you make in your life. Let Him be real to your child as she sees you study His Word and walk with Him everyday.

Second Key – Unconditional Love: Make sure that your child knows without a doubt that you love her unconditionally. It is important that she learn to know the difference between your approval and your love for her. It is OK to not approve of everything your child does, but she must always feel that you love her.

Third Key – Unconditional Value: Make sure that your child knows without a doubt that you value her unconditionally. If your child feels that you will only give her value and worth if she "earns" it, she will have a tendency to become a perfectionist. She begins to believe that any love or value given to her must be earned. This can also impact her relationship with God.

Fourth Key - Set Boundaries: This is often the most difficult for Christian parents to enforce. It is critical to your child that she has boundaries. She does not need another friend, what she needs is someone that knows what is appropriate for her age. Dr. Dobson, with Focus on the Family, states that when a child is born she has zero control of her life and the parent has one hundred percent control. As she grows older it is important to begin giving her more and more control for the decisions in her life. By the time she is eighteen years old, she should be one hundred percent in control of her decisions and you as her parent have moved to the position of friend, counselor, and advisor.

Stress in Your Childs Life

I challenge you as a parent to limit the amount of stimulation your child experiences. Over-stimulation is a growing problem not only with children but also for all of us. Over-stressed children are prone to violence, depression, obesity, increased suicide and anxiety. In fact, anxiety and depression is occurring at younger ages than ever before.

Stress can be caused by many things. A few of them are: too much time spent on video games, computers, listening to headphones with non-soothing music, moving, changing schools, a death in the family, conflict in the home or conflict at school. In fact, the most damaging stress often comes from "good things" in life.

Things that will help you assess your child stress levels are:

1. His immune system – Is he having more colds, flu or headaches than before? Does he seem tired and irritable all the time?

2. Does he seem more sensitive to pain? Will he say he hurts with injuries he used to ignore?

3. Is he having more difficulty in social settings? For instance, does he get into fights or receive detentions at school?

4. Has his behavior with you and his brothers and sisters gotten worse? Is he quick tempered and sensitive to what everyone says to him?

What Do You Owe Your Children

What do you owe your children? By following the steps outlined at the beginning of this chapter, you will give your children what they need.

A. Sense of personal worth by letting them know you value them regardless of their performance.

B. Consistent discipline which provides the structure that they need to feel secure and loved. This includes limiting the amount of time they spend on the internet, texting and playing games on the computer.

C. Privacy and respect are necessary components for your child's growth. However, always reserve the right to come into their room for inspection if you feel something harmful may be going on. Never let a child have an internet connection in their bedroom.

D. The courage to say no to the child's request to reduce the "down time" they need. Many good things will interfere with your child achieving their best. Limit them to one or no more than two activities at a time. Let them choose but they need limits set. For example, they can be in soccer and the school play but only two things. Limiting to one activity is even better.

E. Model Christ before them in your life. Let them observe that you do not take things from work unless authorized. I heard a story about a father that was called to school because his son had been caught stealing an ink pen. The father response was," I don't know why he would do that I can get him all he needs at my work."

F. Have "floor time" with your children at least once per week. Floor time is when you do what ever your child wants to do for twenty to thirty minutes with no criticism or instruction. Just have fun together. This can be blocks with young children and games or video with older children.

G. Make sure your child gets at least eight hours of sleep each night and nine hours is better. Also, make sure they have time to be quiet. One way you will know you are doing the right thing is when they come to you and tell you they are bored.

Stress Free Discipline

Here are five rules to help you have stress free discipline in your home.

1. Good discipline gives adequate warning ahead of time as to "What behavior is not acceptable." For example, if your five year old tracks mud on your clean floor, if you have never told him that is not acceptable, then he does not deserve negative consequences.

2. Establish a consequence for unacceptable behavior. Never make threats you do not intend to carry out. A good consequence for younger children is a time out. The time out should be appropriate for their age. For example, a five year old needs a five minute time out, but it does not begin until the child is setting quietly.

3. Always give warnings to the child that they are drifting into unacceptable behavior. Young

children have a very short memory about rules and may forget.

4. It is important to apply consequences consistently. Never threaten consequences you are not willing to enforce.

5. Make allowances for forgiveness and reconciliation. Make sure that the child understands that although you are not pleased with their action, you still love and value them unconditionally. After the punishment is completed, it is important to give the child a hug or a pat on the shoulder to reassure them of your love for them.

Chapter Ten

Discipline and Pruning
- My Experiences

> First, I went to God and said "Stand back and look at what I am going to do for You!" When that attempt fail completely I went to God and said "Why don't You and I be partners?" When that attempt failed completely I went to God and said, "Why don't You use this clay vessel to serve You as You will? And He said I will do that and He has.

In my counseling sessions I occasionally share some of my life lessons with clients. They have ask me include a few of them in this book. Let me declare before I start this task that I am still in the middle of this wonderful adventure and have a very long way to go to get to where my Lord wants me to be. If I ever have any doubt of how far I still need to go, all I need to do is ask my wonderful wife of 43 years and she helps me remember.

To begin, I have no doctrinal issues that I am willing to argue a bought except what I call the essential doctrines as I understand them. These are the doctrines that I think you must believe to live in heaven with God the Father, God the Son and God the Holy Spirit. Briefly they are as follows:

1. We are all sinners in need of a savior.

2. Jesus Christ is the second part of the Trinity and is eternal.

3. Jesus was born of the virgin Mary

4. He lived a perfect sinless life.

5. He died on the cross to pay for our sins.

6. He physically rose from the grave on the third day.

7. If we truly accept Jesus Christ as our Lord and Savior we will spend eternity in heaven with the Trinity.

What are Discipline and Pruning?

Briefly, in John Chapter 15, Jesus begins a teaching on how God works with his children to help us become who He wants us to become. For a more complete discussion of this I recommend Bruce Wilkerson's book *Secrets of the Vine*.

Discipline is applied when we are in gross sin and rebellion. We know we are doing something that is not pleasing to our heavenly Father, but we enjoy the sin more than we enjoy fellowship with Him. This is not something that any earthly father would allow, so why would we think that God the Father would not take steps to bring us back into fellowship with Him? What may happen in this situation is that God removes His protective covering from us and allows our enemy, Satan, to bring evil into our lives.

Does that mean that every time someone experiences problems with Satan that they are in gross sin? Absolutely not, we live in a fallen world and Satan hates all God's children. However, if it seems like Satan is causing you more problems than usual, hit your knees and ask God to show you if there is sin in your life He wants you to deal with. If He does, then repent (turn away from it) and ask Him to forgive you, then forgive yourself and move on in your walk with Him.

Pruning is applied when God desires to move us to a higher level of "fruitfulness" for Him. He wants us to deepen our relationship with Him and learn to trust Him even more. One of the problems with pruning is that it feels just like discipline. That is why it is so important to determine that any gross sin and rebellion issues have been addressed. Once you are sure God is not disciplining you, your job is to find out what is He wanting to accomplish in your life. Determine what is blocking you from moving to a higher place with Him and begin repositioning the issue in your life priorities.

In pruning God normally wants us to take something that is good and replace it with something that is better.

For example, a wife may love her husband and children more than she loves God. She never would think of it that way, but God knows her heart. What she has inadvertently done is make her husband and children an idol in her life. God will prune her to remind her that He allows no one to be an idol in the life of His children. It is important that she have her priorities correct: God first, husband second, children third, work fourth.

Does God Want Us to Succeed?

First major pruning

In 1982 I sold a business that I had built from the ground up for a profit of $482,000. For a small town boy that was a great deal of money. I had been studying the health, wealth and prosperity message faithfully for a few years at this time and was sure that God was going to allow me to be a major financial resource for His kingdom.

I basically went to Him and said, "Watch what I am going to do for you now, my Father!" Please understand that I loved God at that time with all my heart and truly wanted to serve Him. But I was about to learn a lesson about the sovereignty of God.

We were living in a beautiful home on a lake in Oklahoma with a panoramic view. We lived just down the street from my parents and it was wonderful for my children to have their grandparents so close. We had a great church we were active in and were supporting several ministries. It looked like God was on board with my plans one hundred percent.

Within two years I had turned that $482,000 into $10,000 and was confused and angry with God. I had made all the "right" confessions and believed that I knew God's plan for my life. Why was God not doing what I thought He should do?

I was able to obtain a job in Houston working for a man that had worked for me years earlier. So I moved my family from that beautiful home into a duplex apartment in a less desirable part of Houston, Texas. As I traveled an hour each way to work and home I had the opportunity to listen to Christian teachings on the radio. This is where God began to do a radical work in my life. These teachers began to show me that God is beyond my ability to understand except at the most basic levels. What I had to do was trust Him as a child and let his will work in my life.

Second Major Pruning

After working in Houston for about five years the Lord providentially provided me a job with a major oil company and a substantial raise in salary. In the eleven years I worked there I received steady pay raises and had saved about $300,000 when I retired at fifty six years old. I was now smart enough to know that I wanted God to be my partner as I became a major financial resource for His kingdom.

Through a number of business decisions I was able to make that $300,000 become $12,000 in about four years. However, by this time I knew enough to turn to

Him and say, "What is this pruning about and what are You teaching me?"

He led me to understand that He was not looking for partners but for bond servants. People that love Him enough to give themselves and everything they have to His service.

Once I understood that, amazing things began to happen in my life. I already had a degree in mechanical engineering and was able to obtain a masters and doctorate in Christian counseling from a seminary. I opened my counseling office in 2004 on a donation only basis. I have not grown financially rich but I have been blessed to see many people grow in their relationship with the Lord as they allow me to coach and cheerlead them on their journey with Him.

Do I regret the loss of over $700,000? Not for one minute do I regret it. It was the best money I ever spent. There is no way to place a value on the closeness I feel to my heavenly Father as I understand that He knows what is best for me.

Each of us has unique ways that God can prune us to become who we should be in Him. Let me encourage you to trust in His providential care for you. He truly is your loving Heavenly Father.

Chapter Eleven

Becoming a Lay Christian Counselor

Introduction to the Course

The church is in desperate need of godly counselors who will give advice from the Scripture to its membership. The techniques I outline below are not difficult. In my opinion, there are two important qualifications for being a lay Christian counselor. One is a good understanding of the Scriptures. Equally important is the ability to establish a relationship with the person you are trying to counsel. Many people in the church feel the call of God on their lives to come alongside and help but feel unprepared to do that job. This training is for you.

Lay Christian Counseling Training

Although there are many reasons for the destructive behavior people exhibit, there is only one solution –

developing the ability to "see" ourselves as Jesus Christ sees us. We must develop the "Christ-like" self-image.

Mark 12:30, 31 "you shall love the Lord your God with all your heart, with all your soul, with your entire mind, and with all your strength. This is the first commandment. The second, like it, is this: <u>You shall love your neighbor as yourself</u>." (Note – it is critical that we know God in a loving manner. We cannot extend agape (unconditional) love above the level that we think God loves us. That is why it is so important to realize how much God loves us!)

Romans 12:2 "And do not be conformed to this world, but be transformed by the <u>renewing of your mind</u>, that you may prove what is that good and acceptable and perfect will of God."

<u>Mission:</u> To help the Christian counselor become equipped to help the counselee identify the "Christ-like" self-Image he needs to develop.

<u>Vision:</u> To teach this counseling technique to churches, Christian organizations and qualified believers across the US and increase the joy and fulfillment of the believers of the Lord Jesus Christ and therefore increase the effectiveness of their counseling activities.

<u>Value:</u> As believers in Christ learn that their significance and security reside in Him, they will live a life reflecting the Fruit of the Spirit (Galatians 5: 22, 23) and draw more people into a relationship with our beloved Savior.

We need to ask ourselves a question as we begin these training sessions. Why do the people of the church, for the most part, look just like the lost world around us? Our divorce rate is about the same, we chase after money and possessions, and we don't appear to the world to have any more joy than they do. Why have we accepted Salvation and yet not experienced the Love, Joy and Peace that the Scripture talks about? Much of the answer is in the following two statements.

1. "For as a man thinks in his heart, so is he": Proverbs 23:7a.

2. Many believers in the church today have a damaged self-image, and it is wreaking havoc on God's people.

What you are going to begin learning today is how to help someone change (1) their self-image to align with the self-image of the Lord Jesus Christ. You want to help the counselee go from a "worldly self-image" to the "Christ-like" self-image; and (2) help them learn to obtain the majority of their security (unconditional love) and significance (value) from their relationship with the Lord Jesus. To accomplish this mission, you need to be grounded in the Word of God and live to serve and worship Him.

The first thing that *must* be established in the person who wants to become a Christian counselor is the absolute authority of the Word of God. If the counselor cannot or will not accept the absolute supremacy of the Word of God in all situations he will encounter, then he should not desire to be a Christian counselor. The only hope the counselee has of succeeding in his counseling sessions is that the authority of the Word of God is presented without compromise by the counselor. In addition, all counseling activities must be "bathed" in prayer and the counselor must remember that the real work is done by the Holy Spirit. You are only a tool to encourage (cheerlead) and teach (coach) the client and should spend time on your knees making sure you don't confuse yourselves with who is the real Healer; the One who creates the "Slow Motion Miracles." Only through the work of the Holy Spirit can any meaningful healing occur. In addition, it is critical that all information between the counselor and the counselee be held in strict confidence. (There is an exception to this confidential requirement if criminal actions are being committed.)

To be an effective counselor, you must develop the ability to be an "active listener." What is an "active listener"? It is a counselor who is more interested in what the counselee is saying and the information he is conveying than in what the counselor will say when it is his turn to talk. Information is conveyed by three methods during a face-to-face conversation. (1) The words that are spoken represent about 20% of the information, (2) The inflection of the voice will convey about 40% of the information, and (3) The body language of the person will convey about 40% of the information. This is why the most effective counseling is accomplished in a face-to-face situation.

(1) Listen to the words being used; are they "loaded" with emotional overtones? Examples would be words such as

anger, rage, despair, hate, or other words that express strong emotions. Also be sensitive to words that carry no emotion at all and may indicate a counselee who is hiding his feelings.

(2) The tone or inflection of the voices of the counselee and the counselor will transmit a great deal of information. Think a moment about two ways you can say "Honey, come here." One will indicate a warm request to someone that is loved and another can transmit a harsh command to obey. It is important that the counselor not be shocked or condemning about information that is shared. The counselor will, at the appropriate time, begin to correct sinful behavior with Scriptural applications, but first a relationship of trust and compassion must be developed.

(3) The body language is something most of us are not even conscious of as we read it. Begin to be aware of the information the counselee is giving you in his body language. His body language will give you information about how willing he is to receive your input and how open he is to change. It will tell you if he is excited or fearful of change. Also, the counselee will be reading your body language, so be sure to keep an open, friendly, caring, and interested posture. It is best if you do not let anything be between you and the counselee, such as a desk. The counselor does not want to come across as placing any barriers between himself and the person he is working with. It is critical that the counselor is seen as interested in helping the counselee reestablish a relationship with the Lord that reflects the Fruit of the Spirit.

Changing the Self-Image/Self-Worth Beliefs of the Counselee

Self-image and self-worth are interchangeable terms that describe how people perceive themselves. It does not matter how others value your worth; it only matters how much you value yourself. At times I think the church has lost much of its effectiveness because many of the people who have received Jesus as their Savior do not realize what great value they are to God. The counselor's work, with the guidance of the Holy Spirit, is to help the counselee understand who he is in Christ Jesus and how incredibly valuable he is to God.

Our self-image comes from our view of our significance and security. Problems begin to arise when we obtain significance or security from any other source that the Lord Jesus. Men are prone to lean more heavily toward the significance area (their purpose, importance, job, impact). Women are more prone to lean toward the security area (love – unconditionally and consistently expressed). Both are necessary. Everyone and everything in this world will let you down or disappoint you from time to time. There is only one person who will never let you down and that is Jesus. Therefore, to secure the significance and security we need to experience the Fruit of the Spirit, we must learn to place all our trust and hope in the promises of the Word of God.

1. Explain to the counselee about his "picture album": We all hold within our subconscious mind a picture album of who we are – this is what comprises our "self-image." Many things have influenced this image of ourselves as

we have walked through life. We live in a fallen world with all of its evil influences. Because of them we have all developed many destructive and incorrect pictures and have placed them in our album. This is exactly what the enemy of your soul wants you to do (Rev 12:10). These negative pictures make us less effective for the God whom we serve. We will begin to learn today what pictures our loving Father wants us to have in our album.

2. Only one person has a perfect self-image and that was the Lord Jesus who was God made flesh and dwelt among us (John 1:14). Jesus, who was fully God and fully man was tempted in every way we are (Matt 4:1), but He did not have our "sin nature" and was therefore able to develop only Godly pictures to go into His human picture album. The counselee, as child of the King and joint heir with Christ (Rom. 8:17), has the ability to move his self-image to be in line with the Savior. This is a life-long job, but well worth the effort for the here and now and the hereafter. Every believer in the Lord Jesus Christ is worthy to receive spiritual prosperity from God.

3. It is vital that the counselee control the thoughts of his heart by the use of self-talk and visualization of the desired goal (Matt. 11:29; 12:34-37). <u>Please note</u> that the self-talk and visualization I am speaking about is not the same as what the new age and eastern religions refer to in their teachings. Their teachings are in the best case humanistic and can be potentially demonic. Any visualization or self-talk that does not emphasize the Word of God and His love for you is to be avoided. (Note: self-talk is the continual conversation a person has with himself in his mind. In many people, this self-talk is

anything but "Christ-centered" and is very negative and destructive.)

4. The assignment for the counselee is to write on 3-inch by 5-inch cards his "self-talk" for a week. Then the counselor will review this "self-talk" with the counselee and develop "response" cards to counter the worldly self-talk with Godly self-talk. Every time a worldly thought enters the counselee's mind, he is to immediately read the "Christ-like" statement on the card to reinforce his value as a child of God. This is the first and most important step in changing a person's damaged "worldly" self-image to the "Christ-like" self-image. The sub-conscious mind believes whatever it is told, so what people say to themselves is critical.

5. It is important to realize that even scripturally correct teaching will not automatically clear up any wrong ideas someone may have about God's desire to bless him. The problem is, even scripturally correct truth cannot always penetrate a self-image that is filled with misinformation about who he is in Jesus Christ and what his rights and privileges are as a child of God. For example if you pour pure water through a contaminated filter, the water will be come out polluted and unhealthy. It is the same when the counselee filters God's truth through concepts that are incorrect. As a child of the King, it is vital that his desires be in line with the great commandment: "Love God and Love your fellow man" (Matt. 22: 36-40), and he cannot truly love others until he understands how much our Heavenly Father loves him and wants him to succeed. It is useful if you can help the counselee determine where the negative "pictures" have come from.

As he identifies these sources of negative self-images within himself, he will be able to realize that the people who put the negative ideas in there were not God and did not represent the things that God thinks about the counselee.

6. The counselee's current circumstances are not fixed. He doesn't deny them, but he doesn't let it fix his future circumstances. Current circumstances are a starting point the counselee moves from to his new reality. To respond wisely to his circumstances, he must allow the Word to override the erroneous input from his perceived "truth" and bring it to the Truth in the Word of God. The counselee may try to defend such things as "I am unworthy, unloved, unnecessary" or several other un-words, but these are all lies that Satan uses to keep him from the promises of God. His old nature is his problem but Satan will use it to keep him defeated. *If the client he changes the way he thinks, he will change the way he acts!* If he changes the belief, the performance follows. As Henry Ford said, "Whether you think you can or you think you can't - you're probably right!

7. *It is critically important that the counselee daily use Godly self-affirmation of whom he is in Christ Jesus.* (Examples are contained in Appendix II.) He must learn to trust and obey God's Word and daily die to self and focus on His desires for him. God is only interested in how the counselee's relationship with Him is growing; everything else is used by God to help the counselee in that growth. The counselee may think that God gave him a task to accomplish and that is what He is interested in him doing, when in fact, He gave him the task as a tool He

uses to draw the counselee closer to Him. Our heavenly Father may not care at all if the counselee ever completes the task as long as he continues to deepen his relationship with Him.

8. The question you will often hear from clients is, "How do I learn to make Jesus the major source for my basic needs?" Or to state it another way, "How can I learn to let Jesus fill my Love & Value tank?" There are at least three things that can be done.

The first step is the most important. You must decide that the Word of God is true, regardless of how things look or how you feel. This step gives you a "stake in the ground" to anchor steps two and three.

Step two is beginning to change the negative pictures in your subconscious photo album. Those pictures stop you from believing that God loves you unconditionally and considers your worth to be beyond value.

The third step is to begin to do things as an offering to your heavenly Father. You no longer expect rewards or payoffs when you do things for others. Instead you trust your Father in Heaven to meet your basic needs. When you do the act of offering to the Lord, say to yourself: "Lord, I am doing this as an offering to You. I am not expecting anything back from the person I am doing it for; I am looking to You to meet my need for security and significance. This act of sacrifice does at least three things:

(1) It takes the pressure off the relationship with the person you are doing an act of service to because you are not expecting anything back from them.

(2) Based on the principle of sowing and reaping in the Bible, you are giving God something to multiply back to you to meet your basic needs.

(3) God will pour into your life a 30-, 60- or 100-fold return on what you did as a true offering to Him. No matter how small or insignificant you may think the offering is; God is looking at the attitude of your heart, not the size of your offering.

Remember, as your "love & value tank" begins to fill with the unconditional love and great value that God gives you, less and less pressure will be placed on the relationships around you. In fact, God's agape love and value will overflow out of you and spill over into other lives.

9. Wrong thinking patterns: A pattern is used to mold what ever is poured into its shape. When patterns of thinking are locked into the counselee's mind, thoughts will come out in a biased manner nearly every time. Any pattern of thinking that cannot be verified with Christ-like thinking and the Word of God will always bring defeat. That is why the counselee is told to renew his mind with the Word. (Rom. 12:2) These thinking patterns become a belief. Correct Christian beliefs will fortify and strengthen his faith. However, it is possible for even Christians to have wrong or distorted beliefs

that can lead them into a distorted perception of "truth." Beliefs, therefore, are the engine that drives the way the counselee acts and reacts to most situations. Any type of negative behavior such as anger, cruelty, unbelief, sarcasm or unforgiveness can become a habitual form of behavior. God's understanding and mercy will never excuse these negative behaviors and they must be defeated with the help of the Holy Spirit before the counselee will be able to experience the fullness of God's blessings.

10. The subconscious Mind acts like a busy artist, which captures and stores its version of the "circumstances" as they happen. It paints its own pictures of "the truth" about the person, which he begins to believe is the "real" person. Since pictures are the most vivid when they are young, they often have the most impact on the person's idea of who they are. No matter how detrimental the pictures are, the counselee is stuck with them until he consciously decide to repaint the canvas. In addition, due to the egocentric nature of children and young people, everything that happens to them is about them and is their fault.

11. Lou Tice in his book *Smart Talk* introduces the concept of the creative subconscious. It is a force within the subconscious that reviews the pictures it observes in the subconscious mind and then sets out to recreate the same circumstances in the real world. It will maintain order by projecting the subconscious's ideas of "the truth" and convince the counselee that the pictures are "just like me." It maintains whatever level of worth that is recorded.

12 The counselee must change the self-image in his internal picture album one picture at a time using the promises of the Word of God.

- "I have great value because God loved me enough to die in my place."

- "People will like me because I treat them like they are my beloved brothers and sisters in the Lord."

- "I succeed in what I attempt to accomplish because I have the Holy Spirit guiding my steps."

There is a direct relationship between the quality of his knowledge and his understanding of God's promises. God's Word living in his heart will determine what he will hold in his mind and the way he leads his life. Change the inside and the outside will change! To release the potential of the counselee, he needs to correct the misinformation that he has stored about life. He must not accept the lies of Satan but accept what his heavenly Father says about him.

13. *Overcoming negative beliefs = overcoming a lack of faith in God's promises for the counselee.* When no problem is identified then no feedback occurs and there is no correction of the internal picture. The counselee must identify his negative beliefs to overcome them. He needs to begin to listen to his internal conversation with himself. Negative belief = lack of faith. Questions for the counselee to ask himself:

a. Does the counselee constantly "beat" himself up with internal condemnation and guilt?

    b. Does the counselee have only negative thoughts about others?

    c. When given a choice, does the counselee ever choose to think the best about a person's action?

    d. Does the counselee turn over to God the cares and troubles of the day and leave them there?

14. People tend to behave and become like the image they hold in their subconscious mind. The counselee may extend his beliefs to other people and stereotype them. For instance, you may hear him say, "All Christians are judgmental." This will cause the person who made that statement to avoid believers in Christ. In essence, "People will either "live up" or "live down" to the counselee's expectations! The counselee must stop reliving every mistake he has ever made – "If we confess our sins, He is faithful and just to forgive our sins and cleans us from all unrighteousness," 1 John 1:9. He must forgive himself just as God has forgiven him! (Phil. 3:13)

15. The counselee's automatic pilot is his self-image and his self-image must always be growing in its understanding of how much God loves him and wants him to succeed. It determines the direction he will lean, positive or negative. *How does the counselee change his self-image? By controlling and changing his confession! The counselee should confess only what the Word of God says about him.*

- God loves me so much He sacrificed His own Son to cover my sins , (John 3:16)

- I am His child and very precious to Him, (Romans 8:16)

- I can do all things through Christ who strengthens me, (Philippians 4:13)

- Greater is He that is in me than he (the devil) who is in the world, (1st John 4:4)

- Beloved I wish that you may prosper and be in health as your soul prospers, (3 John 1:2)

- Seek first the Kingdom of God and His righteousness and all things will be added to me, (Mathew 6:33)

16. Constructive self-talk is "God-talk." "God-talk" is the continual dialogue the counselee must use to affirm God's love and provision for himself. It is the raw material from which the counselee manufactures his self-image. The counselee's subconscious believes what it is told. It must be instructed to act according to what the Word of God says about it. *The counselee cannot change an event, but he can change his interpretation of the event by controlling his self-talk.* The counselee will move toward and become what he thinks about. His present thoughts are the seeds that determine his future actions!

May God bless your efforts and remember all the real work is done by the power of the Holy Spirit working through you. To God Be the Glory!

Note: Copies of this teaching seminar may be reproduced as long as they are distributed free of charge. It is a gift from God and should be used as such.

Dr. Vick L. Newsom, D. Min. C. C.

WWW.GlorytoGod.net   417-334-8777

Third Printing

May all honor and glory be given to my beloved Father in heaven and to His son, my Savior and friend, and to the Holy Spirit who points us to Jesus!

From His bond servant – Vick L. Newsom

A FINAL THOUGHT - A CARD TO CARRY

Make yourself a card you can laminate and carry in your wallet or purse. Everytime you feel the devil climbing on your back, take it out and read it!

My favorite Scripture is John 3:16 personalized to read: God loved me so much that He willingly came to earth and died for me. What great worth I must have in God's eyes for Him to love me so much. I am indeed blessed in my coming in and my going out.

You pick your own or use the one above. The point is, do not let your enemy, Satan, get the jump on you again. God Bless you!

APPENDIX ONE

The "Roman Road" provides excellent tools for helping someone understand their need for a personal relationship with the Lord Jesus Christ. If a person indicates they are interested in knowing more about why Jesus should be their Lord, I "walk" the Roman Road with them and we discuss it.

Roman Road

1. Roman 3:23 "for all have sinned, and fall short of the glory of God;"

2. Roman 6:23 "For the wages of sin is death; but the free gift of God is eternal life in Christ Jesus our Lord."

3. Roman 5:8-9 "But God commends his own love toward us, in that, while we were yet sinners, Christ died for us. Much more then, being now justified by his blood, shall we be saved from the wrath [of God] through him."

4. Roman 5:1 "Being therefore justified by faith, we have peace with God through our Lord Jesus Christ;"

5. Roman 10:9-10 "because if you shall confess with your mouth Jesus [as] Lord, and shall believe in your heart that God raised him from the dead, you shall be saved: for with the heart man believeth unto righteousness; and with the mouth confession is made unto salvation."

6. Roman 10:13 "for, Whosoever shall call upon the name of the Lord shall be saved."

7. Roman 8:1 "There is therefore now no condemnation to them that are in Christ Jesus."

After we discuss the Roman Road, I ask them if they would like to make Jesus their Savior. If they say yes, then I have them repeat a prayer after me.

My blessed Father in heaven, I confess that I am a sinner in need of a Savior. I believe that Jesus is Your only begotten Son and that He died for my sins and you raised Him from the dead on the third day. I invite You Lord Jesus to come into my heart and I accept You as my Lord and My Savior. In Your name I pray. Amen

After he accepts Jesus as Savior, I encourage him to get into a Bible believing church and begin the most exciting adventure of his life, developing the "Christ-like" self-image.

APPENDIX TWO

Useful Scriptures for Counseling

KJV and NKJV

ANXIETY AND WORRY

Matthew 6:31, 32; "Therefore take no thought, saying, What shall we eat? Or, What shall we drink? or, Wherewithal shall we be clothed? (For after all these things do the Gentiles seek:) for your heavenly Father knows that you have need of all these things."

Philippians 4:6, 7; "Be anxious for nothing; but in every thing by prayer and supplication with thanksgiving let your requests be made known unto God. And the peace of God, which passes all understanding, shall keep your hearts and minds through Christ Jesus."

Philippians 4:19;"But my God shall supply all your need according to His riches in glory by Christ Jesus."

I Peter 5:7; "Casting all your care upon Him; for He cares for you."

BEREAVEMENT AND LOSS

Deuteronomy 31:8; "And the Lord, He it is that does go before you; He will be with you, He will not fail you, neither forsake you: fear not, neither be dismayed."

Psalm 27:10; "When my father and my mother forsake me, then the Lord will take me up,"

II Corinthians 6:10; "As sorrowful, yet always rejoicing; as poor, yet making many rich: as having nothing, yet possessing all things."

Philippians 3:8; "You doubtless, and I count all things but loss for the excellency of the knowledge of Christ Jesus my Lord: for whom I have suffered the loss of all things, and do count them but dung, that I may win Christ."

COMFORT

Psalm 23:4 – "Yea, though I walk through the valley of the shadow of death, I will fear no evil: for You art with me; Your rod and Your staff they comfort me."

Matthew 5:4 – "Blessed are they that mourn; for they shall be comforted."

Matthew 11:28-30 – "Come unto me, all you that Labour and are heavy laden, and I will give you rest. Take my yoke upon you, and learn of me; for I am meek and lowly in heart: and you shall find rest unto your souls. For my yoke is easy, and my burden is light."

John 14:16, 18 – "And I will pray the Father, and He shall give you another Comforter, that He may abide with you for ever; I will not leave you comfortless: I will come to you."

II Corinthians 1:3, 4, - "Blessed be God, even the Father of our Lord Jesus Christ, the Father of mercies, and the God of all comfort. Who comforts us in all our tribulations, that we may be able to comfort them which are in any trouble, by the comfort wherewith we ourselves are comforted of God."

CONFIDENCE (Developing)

Psalm 27:3 – "Though a host should encamp against me, my heart shall not fear: though war should rise against me, in this will I be confident."

Proverbs 3:26 – "For the Lord shall be Your confidence, and shall keep your foot from being taken."

Proverbs 14:26 – "In the fear of the Lord is strong confidence; and His children shall have a place of refuge."

Mark 9:23 – "Jesus said to him, 'If you can believe, all things are possible to him who believes.'"

Galatians 6:9 – "And let us not be weary in well doing; for in due season we shall reap, it we faint not."

Romans 8:37 – "Yet in all these things we are more than conquerors through Him who loved us."

Matthew 21:22 - "And whatever things you ask in prayer, believing, you will receive."

Philippines 4:13 – "I can do all things through Christ which strengthens me."

Philippians 1:6 – "Being confident of this very thing, that He which has begun a good work in you will perform it until the day of Jesus Christ;"

Hebrews 10:35 – "Cast not away therefore your confidence, which has great recompense of reward."

I Peter 2:9 – "But you are a chosen generation, a royal priesthood, a holy nation, a peculiar people; that you should show forth the praises of Him who has called you out of darkness into His marvelous light."

<u>DANGER (Protection from)</u>

Psalm 23:4 – "Yea, though I walk through the valley of the shadow of death, I will fear no evil; for You are with me; Your rod and Your staff they comfort me."

Psalm 32:7 – "You art my hiding place, You shall preserve me from trouble; You shall compass me about with songs of deliverance."

Psalm 34:7 – "The angel of the Lord encamps round about them that fear him, and delivers them."

Psalm 34:17 – "The righteous cry, and the Lord hears, and delivers them out of all their troubles."

Psalm 34:19 – "Many are the afflictions of the righteous: but the Lord delivers him out of them all."

Psalm 91:1 – "He that dwells in the secret place of the Most High shall abide under the shadow of the Almighty."

Psalm 91:11 – "For He shall give His angels charge over you, to keep you in all your ways."

Psalm 121:8 – "The Lord shall preserve your going out and your coming in from this time forth, and even for evermore."

Romans 14:8 – "For whether we live, we live unto the Lord; and whether we die, we die unto the Lord: whether we live therefore, or die, we are the Lord's."

DEATH

Psalm 23:4 – "Yea, though I walk through the valley of the shadow of death I will fear no evil: for You are with me; Your rod and Your staff they comfort me."

Psalm 116:15 – "Precious in the sight of the Lord is the death of his saints."

Romans 14:8 – "For whether we live, we live unto the Lord; and whether we die, we die unto the Lord: whether we live therefore, or die, we are the Lord's."

II Corinthians 5:1 – "For we know that if our earthly house of this tabernacle were dissolved, we have a building of God, an house not made with hands, eternal in the heavens".

Philippians 1:21 – "For me to live is Christ, and to die is gain."

I Thessalonians 5:9, 10 – "For God has not appointed us to wrath, but to obtain salvation by our Lord Jesus Christ, Who died for us, that, whether we wake or sleep, we should live together with Him."

Hebrew's 9:27 – "And as it is appointed unto men once to die, but after this the judgment"

Revelation 21:4 – "And God shall wipe away all tears from their eyes; and there shall be no more death, neither sorrow, nor crying, neither shall there be any more pain: for the former things are passed away."

DIFFICULTIES (Discipline through)

Romans 8:28 "And we know that all things work together for good to them that love God, to them who are the called according to His purpose."

II Corinthians 4:17 – "For our light affliction, which is but for a moment, works for us a far more exceeding and eternal weight of glory."

Hebrews 5:8 – "Though he was a Son, yet He learned obedience by the things which He suffered;"

Hebrews 12:7 – "If you endure chastening, God deals with you as with sons; for what son is he whom the father chasten not?"

Hebrews 12:11 – "Now no chastening for the present seem to be Joyous, but grievous; nevertheless, afterward it yield the peaceable fruit of righteousness unto them which are exercised thereby."

Revelation 3:19 – "And as many as I love, I rebuke and chasten: be zealous therefore and repent."

DISAPPOINTMENT

Psalm 43:5 – "Why art you cast down, O my soul? and why art you disquieted within me? hope in God: for I shall yet praise Him."

Psalm 55:22 – "Cast your burden upon the Lord, and He shall sustain you: He shall never suffer the righteous to be moved."

John 14:27 – "Peace I leave with you, my peace I give unto you: not as the world giveth, give I unto you. Let not your heart be troubled, neither let it be afraid."

II Corinthians 4:8, 9 – "We are troubled on every side, yet not distressed; we are perplexed, but not in despair; Persecuted, but not forsaken; cast down, but not destroyed;"

DISCOURAGEMENT

Joshua 1:9 – "Have not I commanded you? Be strong and of a good courage; be not afraid, neither be you dismayed: for the Lord Your God is with you whithersoever you go."

Psalm 27:14 – "Wait on the Lord; be of good courage, and He shall strengthen your heart: wait, I say, on the Lord."

Psalm 43:5 – "Why art you cast down, O my soul? and why are you disquieted within me? hope in God: for I shall yet praise Him Who is the health of my countenance, and my God."

John 14:1 – "Let not your heart be troubled: you believe in God, believe also in Me."

John 14:27 – "Peace I leave with you, my peace I give unto you: not as the world giveth, give I unto you. Let not your heart be troubled, neither let it be afraid."

John 16:33 – "These things I have spoken unto you, that in me you might have peace. In the world you shall have tribulation: but be of good cheer; I have overcome the world."

Hebrews 4:16 – "Let us therefore come boldly unto the throne of grace that we may obtain mercy, and find grace to help in time of need."

John 5:14 – "And this is the confidence that we have in Him, that if we ask anything according to His will, He hears us."

FAITH

Romans 4:3 – "For what says the scripture? Abraham believed God, and it was counted unto him for righteousness."

Romans 10:17 – "So then faith comes by hearing, and hearing by the word of God."

Ephesians 2:8, 9 – "For by grace are you saved through faith; and that not of yourselves; it is the gift of God: Not of works, lest any man should boast."

Hebrews 11:1 – "Now faith is the substance of things hoped for, the evidence of things not seen."

Hebrews 11:6 – "But without faith it is impossible to please Him: for he that cometh to God must believe that He is, and that He rewards them that diligently seek Him."

Hebrews 12:2 – "Looking unto Jesus the author and finisher of our faith; Who for the joy that was set before Him endured the cross, despising the shame, and is set down at the right hand of the throne of God."

James 1:3 – "Knowing this, that the trying of your faith works patience."

James 1:5, 6 – "If any of you lack wisdom, let him ask of God that giveth to all men liberally, and upbraideth not; and it shall be given him. But let him ask in faith, nothing wavering. For he that wavers is like a wave of the sea driven with the wind and tossed."

I Peter 1:7 – "That the trial of your faith, being much more precious than of gold that perish, though it be tried with fire, might be found unto praise and honor and glory at the appearing of Jesus Christ."

FEAR

Psalm 27:1 – "The Lord is my light and my salvation; whom shall I fear? the Lord is the strength of my life; of whom shall I be afraid?"

Psalm 56:11 – "In God have I put my trust: I will not be afraid what man can do unto me."

Proverbs 3:2.5 – "Be not afraid of sudden fear, neither of the desolation of the wicked, when it cometh."

John 14:27 – "Peace I leave with you, my peace I give unto you; not as the world gives, give I unto you. Let not your heart be troubled, neither let it be afraid."

Romans 8:31 – "What shall we then say to these things? If God be for us, who can be against us?"

II Timothy 1:7 – "For God has not given us the spirit of fear; but of power, and of love, and of a sound mind."

I John 4:18 – "There is no fear in love; but perfect love cast out fear: because fear has torment. He that fears is not made perfect in love."

FORGIVENESS OF SIN

Psalm 32:5 – "I acknowledged my sin unto You, and mine iniquity have I not hid. I said, I will confess my transgressions unto the Lord: and You forgave the iniquity of my sin."

Psalm 103:3 – "Who forgives all your iniquities; Who heals all our diseases;"

Psalms 28:13 – "He that covers his sins shall not prosper: but who confess and forsake them shall have mercy."

Isaiah 1:18 – "Come now, and let us reason together, saith the Lord: though your sins be as scarlet, they shall be as white as snow; though they be red like crimson, they shall be as wool."

I John 1:9 – "If we confess our sins. He is faithful and just to forgive us our sins, and to cleanse us from all unrighteousness."

James 5:15, 16 – "And the prayer of faith shall save the sick, and the Lord shall raise him up; and if he has committed sins, they shall be forgiven him. Confess your faults one to another, and pray one for another, that you may be healed. The effectual fervent prayer of a righteous man avails much."

FORGIVING OTHERS

Matthew 5:44-47 – "But I say unto you, love your enemies, bless them that curse you, do good to them that hate you, and pray for them which despitefully use you, and persecute you. That you may be the children of your Father which is in heaven: for He makes His sun to rise on the evil and on the good, and sends rain on the just and on the unjust. For if you love them which love you, what reward have you? Do not even the publicans the same? And if you salute your brethren only, what do you more than others? Do not even the publicans so?"

Matthew 6:12 – "And forgive us our debts, as we forgive our debtors."

Matthew 6:14 – "For if you forgive men their trespasses, your heavenly Father will also forgive you:"

Mark 11:25 – "And when you stand praying, forgive, if you have ought against any: that your Father also which is in heaven may forgive you your trespasses."

Ephesians 4:32 – "And be you kind one to another, tenderhearted, forgiving one another, even as God for Christ's sake has forgiven you."

Colossians 3:13 – "Forbearing one another, and forgiving one another, if any man has a quarrel against any: even as Christ forgave you, so also do you."

FRIENDS AND FRIENDLINESS

Proverbs 18:24 – "A man that has friends must show himself friendly: and there is a friend that sticks closer than a brother."

Matthew 22:39 – "And the second is like unto it, You shall love Your neighbor as Yourself."

John 13:35 – "By this shall all men know that you are my disciples, if you have love one to another."

John 15:13 – "Greater love has no man than this, that a man lay down his life for his friends."

John 15:14 – "You are my friends, if you do whatsoever I command you."

Galatians 6:10 – "As we have therefore opportunity, let us do good unto all men, especially unto them who are of the household of faith."

GROWING SPIRITUALLY

Ephesians 3:17-19 – "That Christ may dwell in your hearts by faith; that you being rooted and grounded in love, May be able to comprehend with all saints what is the breadth, and length, and depth, and height; And to know the love of Christ, which passes knowledge, that you might be filled with all the fullness of God."

Colossians 3:16 – "Let the word of Christ dwell in you richly in all wisdom; teaching and admonishing one another in psalms and hymns and spiritual songs, singing with grace in your hearts to the Lord.

II Timothy 2:15 – "Study to show yourself approved unto God, a workman that needs not to be ashamed, rightly dividing the word of truth."

1 Peter 2:2 – "As newborn babes, desire the sincere milk of the Word, that you may grow thereby."

II Peter 1:5-8 – "But also for this very reason, giving all diligence, add to your faith virtue, to virtue knowledge, to knowledge self-control, to self-control perseverance, to perseverance godliness, to godliness brotherly kindness, and to brotherly kindness love. For if these things are yours and abound, you will be neither barren nor unfruitful in the knowledge of our Lord Jesus Christ."

II Peter 3:18 – "But grow in grace, and in the knowledge of our Lord and Saviour Jesus Christ. To Him be glory both now and for ever. Amen."

GUIDANCE

Psalm 32:8 – "I will instruct you and teach you in the way which you shall go; I will guide you with mine own eyes."

Luke 1:79 – "To give light to them that sit in darkness and in the shadow of death, to guide our feet in the way of peace."

John 16:13 – "Howbeit when He, the Spirit of truth, is come, He will guide you into all truth: for He shall not speak of Himself: but whatsoever He shall hear, that shall He speak; and He will show you things to come."

HELP AND CARE

II Chronicles 16:9 – "For the eyes of the Lord run to and fro throughout the whole earth, to show Himself strong in the behalf of them whose heart is perfect toward Him."

Psalm 34:7 – "The angel of the Lord encamps round about them that fear him and delivers them."

Psalm 37:5 – "Commit your way unto the Lord; trust also in Him; and He shall bring it to pass."

Psalm 37:24 – "Though he falls, he shall not be utterly cast down: for the Lord upholds him with His hand."

Psalm 55:22 – "Cast your burden upon the Lord, and He shall sustain you; He shall never suffer the righteous to be moved."

Psalm 91:4 – "He shall cover you with his feathers, and under His wings shall you trust: His truth shall be your shield and buckler."

Isaiah 54:17 – "No weapon that is formed against you shall prosper; and every tongue that shall rise against you in Judgment you shall condemn. This is the heritage of the servants of the Lord, and their righteousness is of, says the Lord."

Hebrews 4:16 –"Let us therefore come boldly unto the throne of grace, that we may obtain mercy, and find grace to help in time of need."

Hebrews 13:5 – "Let your conversation be without covetousness; and be content with such things as you have; for He has said, I will never leave you, nor forsake you."

Hebrews 13:6 – "So that we may boldly say, The Lord is my helper, and I will not fear what man shall do unto me."

I Peter 5:7 – "Casting all your care upon Him; for He cares for you."

LONELINESS

Psalm 23 – "The Lord is my shepherd; I shall not want. He makes me to lie down in green pastures; He leads me beside the still waters. He restores my soul; He leads me in the paths of righteousness For His name's sake. You, though I walk through the valley of the shadow of death, I will fear no evil; For You are with me; Your rod and Your staff, they comfort me. You prepare a table before me in the presence of my enemies; You anoint my head with oil; My cup runs over. Surely goodness and mercy shall follow me All the days of my life; And I will dwell in the house of the Lord Forever."

Psalm 27:10 – "When my father and my mother forsake me, then the Lord will take me up."

Isaiah 41:10 – "Fear not; for I am with you: be not dismayed; for I am Your God: I will strengthen you; I will help you; I will uphold you with the right hand of my righteousness."

Matthew 28:20 – "Teaching them to observe all things whatsoever I have commanded you: and, lo, I am with you always, even unto the end of the world Amen."

Hebrews 13:5 – "Let your conversation be without covetousness; and be content with such things as you have: for He hath said, I will never leave you, nor forsake you."

LOVE (God's)

John 3:26 – "For God so loved the world, that He gave His only begotten Son, that whosoever believeth in Him should not perish, but have everlasting life."

John 15:9 – "As the Father hath loved me, so have I loved you: continue you in my love."

Romans 5:8 – "But God commends His love toward us, in that while we were yet sinners, Christ died for us."

Romans 8:38, 39 – "For I am persuaded that neither death, nor life, nor angels, nor principalities, nor powers, nor things present, nor things to come, nor height, nor depth, nor any other creature, shall be able to separate us from the love of God, which is in Christ Jesus our Lord."

1 John 3:1 – "Behold, what manner of love the Father hath bestowed upon us, that we should be called the sons of God: therefore, the world knows us not, because it knew Him not."

OBEDIENCE

I Samuel 15:22 – "And Samuel said, Hath the Lord as great delight in burnt offerings and sacrifices, as in obeying the voice of the Lord? Behold, to obey is better than sacrifice, and to hearken than the fat of rams."

Psalm 111:10 – "The fear of the Lord is the beginning of wisdom; a good understanding have all they that do His commandments: His praise endures forever."

Psalm 119:2 – "Blessed are they that keep His testimonies and that seek Him with your whole heart."

Matthew 6:24 – "No man can serve two masters; for either he will hate the one, and love the other; or else he will hold to the one, and despise the other. You will serve God or mammon."

John 14: 15 – "If you love me, keep my commandments."

John 14:21 – "He that has my commandments, and keeps them, he it is that loves me: and he that loves Me shall be loved of my Father, and I will love Him, and will manifest myself to him."

James 2:10 – "For whosoever shall keep the whole law, and yet offend in one point, he is guilty of all,"

1 John 3:22 – "And whatsoever we ask, we receive of Him, because we keep His commandments, and do those things that are pleasing in His sight."

PEACE OF MIND

Isaiah 26:3 – "You will keep him in perfect peace, whose mind is stayed on you: because He trusts in you."

John 14:27 – "Peace I leave with you. My peace I give unto you: not as the world gives, give I unto you. Let not your heart be troubled, neither let it be afraid."

John 16:33 – "These things I have spoken unto you, that in Me you might have peace. In the world you shall have tribulation: but be of good cheer; I have overcome the world."

Roman 5:1 – "Therefore being Justified by faith, we have peace with God through our Lord Jesus Christ."

Philippians 4:7 – "And the peace of God, which passes all understanding, shall keep your hearts and minds though Jesus Christ."

Colossians 3:15 –"And let the peace of God rule in your hearts, to which also you are called in one body; and be thankful."

PERSECUTION

Matthew 5:10, 11 – "Blessed are they which are persecuted for righteousness' sake: for theirs is the kingdom of heaven. Blessed are you, when men shall revile you, and persecute you, and shall say all manner of evil against you falsely, for my sake."

Matthew 10:22 – "And you shall be hated of all men for My Name's sake; but he that endures to the end shall be saved."

Acts 5:41 – "And they departed from the presence of the council, rejoicing that they were counted worthy to suffer shame for His name."

Romans 8:17 – "And if children, then heirs; heirs of God, and joint-heirs with Christ; if so be that we suffer with Him, that we may be also glorified together."

II Timothy 3:12 – "All that will live godly in Christ Jesus shall suffer persecution."

Hebrews 11:25 – "Choosing rather to suffer affliction with the people of God, than to enjoy the pleasures of sin for a season;"

I Peter 2:20 – "For what glory is it, if, when you are buffeted for your faults, you shall take it patiently? but if, when you do well, and suffer for it, you take it patiently, this is acceptable with God."

PRAISE AND GRATITUDE

Psalm 34:1 – "I will bless the Lord at all times: His praise shall continually be in my mouth."

Psalm 50:23 – "Whoso offers praise glorifies me: and to him that orders his conversation aright will I show the salvation of God."

Psalms 51:15 – "O Lord, open you my lips; and my mouth shall show forth Your praise."

Psalm 139:14 – "I will praise you; for I am fearfully and wonderfully made: marvelous are Your works; and that my soul knows right well."

Ephesians 5:20 – "Giving thanks always for all things unto God and the Father in the Name of our Lord Jesus Christ."

Hebrews 13:6 – "So that we may boldly say, The Lord is my helper, and I will not fear what man shall do unto me."

Hebrews 13:15 – "By him therefore let us offer the sacrifice of praise to God continually, that is, the fruit of our lips, giving thanks to His name."

PROVISION

Psalm 34:10 – "The young lions do lack, and suffer hunger: but they that seek the Lord shall not want any good thing."

Psalm 37:3, 4 – "Trust in the Lord, and do good; so shall you dwell in the land, and verily you shall be fed. Delight yourself also in the Lord; and He shall give you the desires of your heart."

Isaiah 58:11 – "And the Lord shall guide you continually, and satisfy your soul in drought, and make fat your bones: and you shall be like a watered garden, and like a spring of water, whose waters fail not."

Matthew 6:33 – "But seek first the kingdom of God, and His righteousness; and all these things shall be added unto you."

II Corinthians 9:8 – "And God is able to make all grace abound toward you; that you, always having all sufficiency in all things, may abound to every good work."

Philippians 4:19 – "But my God shall supply all your need according to His riches in glory by Christ Jesus."

RETURN OF CHRIST

Luke 21:36 – "Watch you therefore, and pray always, that you may be accounted worthy to escape all these things that shall come to pass, and to stand before the Son of Man."

Acts 1:11 – "Which also said. You men of Galilee, why stand you gazing up into heaven? this same Jesus, which is taken up from you into heaven, shall so come in like manner as you have seen Him go into heaven."

I Thessalonians 4:16-18 – "For the Lord Himself shall descend from heaven with a shout, with the voice of the archangel, and with the trump of God: and the dead in Christ shall rise first: Then we which are alive and remain shall be caught up together with them in the clouds, to meet the Lord in the air: and so shall we ever be with the Lord. Wherefore comfort one another with these words."

Titus 2:13 – "Looking for that blessed hope, and the glorious appearing of the great God and our Savior Jesus Christ;"

I John 3:2, 3 – "Beloved, now are we the sons of God, and it does not yet appear what we shall be; but we know that, when He shall appear, we shall be like Him; for we shall see Him as He is. And every man that hath this hope in Him purifies himself, even as he is pure."

SICKNESS

Psalm 41:3 – "The Lord will strengthen him upon the bed of languishing: you will make all his bed in his sickness."

Psalm 103:3 – "Who forgives all your iniquities; Who heals all Your diseases; "

James, 5:15, 16 – "And the prayer of faith shall save the sick, and the Lord shall raise him up; and if he has committed sins, they shall be forgiven him. Confess your faults one to another, and pray one for another, that you may be healed. The effectual fervent prayer of a righteous man avails much."

SIN

Isaiah 53:5, 6 – "But He was wounded for our transgressions, He was bruised for our iniquities: the chastisement of our peace was upon Him; and with His stripes we are healed. All we like sheep have gone astray; we have turned every one to his own way; and the Lord hath laid on Him the iniquity of us all."

Isaiah 59:1, 2 – "Behold, the Lord's hand is not shortened, that it cannot save; neither His ear heavy, that it cannot hear: But your iniquities have separated between you and your God, and your sins have hid His face from you, that He will not hear."

John 8:34 "Jesus answered them, Verily, verily, I say into you. Whosoever commits sin; is the servant of sin."

Romans 3:23 – "For all have sinned, and come short of the glory of God"

Romans 6:23 – "For the wages of sin is death; but the gift of God is eternal life through Jesus Christ our Lord."

Galatians 6:7, 8 – "Be not deceived; God is not mocked; for whatsoever a man sows, that shall he also reap. For he that sows to his flesh shall of the flesh reap corruption; but he that sows to the Spirit shall of the Spirit reap life everlasting."

SORROW

Proverbs 10:22 – "The blessing of the Lord, it makes rich, and He adds no sorrow with it."

Isaiah 53:4 – "Surely He has borne our griefs, and carried our sorrows: yet we did esteem Him stricken, smitten of God, and afflicted."

John 16:22 – "And you now therefore have sorrow: but I will see you again, and your heart shall rejoice, and your joy no man takes from you."

II Corinthians 6:10 – "As sorrowful, yet always rejoicing; as poor, yet making many rich; as having nothing, and yet possessing all things."

I Thessalonians 4:13 – "But I would not have you to be ignorant, brethren, concerning them which are asleep, that you sorrow not, even as others which have no hope."

Revelation 21:4 – "And God shall wipe away all tears from their eyes; and there shall be no more death, neither sorrow, nor crying, neither shall there be any more pain: for the former things are passed away."

STRENGTH

Psalm 27:14 – "Wait on the Lord: be of good courage, and He shall strengthen your heart; wait, I say, on the Lord."

Psalm 28:7 – "The Lord is my strength and my shield: my heart trusted in Him, and I am helped: therefore my heart greatly rejoices; and with my song will I praise Him."

Isaiah 40:29, 31 – "He gives power to the faint; and to them that have no might He increases strength. But they that wait upon the Lord shall renew their strength; they shall mount up with wings as eagles; they shall run, and not be weary; and they shall walk, and not faint."

Isaiah 41:10 – "Fear you not; for I am with you: be not dismayed; for I am Your God: I will strengthen you; you,

I will help you; you, I will uphold you with the right hand of my righteousness."

II Corinthians 12:9 – "And He said unto me, My grace is sufficient for you: for My strength is made perfect in weakness. Most gladly therefore will I rather glory in my infirmities, that the power of Christ may rest upon me."

Philippians 4:13 – "I can do all things through Christ which strengthens me."

SUFFERING

Romans 8:18 – "For I reckon that the sufferings of this present time are not worthy to be compared with the glory which shall be revealed in us."

II Corinthians 1:5 – "For as the sufferings of Christ abound in us, so our consolation also abounds by Christ."

Philippians 1:29 – "For unto you it is given in the behalf of Christ, not only to believe on Him, but also to suffer for His sake."

Philippians 3:10 – "That I may know Him, and the power of His resurrection, and the fellowship of His sufferings, being made conformable unto His death;"

II Timothy 2:12 – "If we suffer, we shall also reign with Him: if we deny Him, He also will deny us:"

I Peter 2:19 – "For this is thankworthy, if a man for conscience toward God endure grief, suffering wrongfully."

I Peter 4:12, 13 – "Beloved, think it not strange concerning the fiery trial which is to try you, as though some strange thing happened unto you; But rejoice, inasmuch as you are partakers of Christ's sufferings; that, when His glory shall be revealed, you may be glad also, with exceeding joy."

1 Peter 4:16 – "Yet it any man suffer as a Christian, let him not be ashamed; but let him glorify God on this behalf."

1 Peter 5:10 – "But the God of all grace, who hath called us unto His eternal glory by Christ Jesus, after that you have suffered a while, make you perfect, establish, strengthen, settle you."

TEMPTATION

I Corinthians 10:12, 13 – "Wherefore let him that thinks he stands take heed lest he fall. There hath no temptation taken you but such as is common to man: but God is faithful, who will not suffer you to be tempted above that you are able; but will with the temptation also make a way to escape, that you may be able to bear it."

Hebrews 2:18 – "For in that He Himself hath suffered being tempted. He is able to succor them that are tempted."

James 1:2, 3 – "My brethren, count it all joy when you fall into divers temptations, knowing this, that the trying of your faith works patience."

James 1:12 – "Blessed is the man that endures temptation: for when he is tried, he shall receive the crown of life, which the Lord hath promised to them that love Him."

James 1:14 – "But every man is tempted, when he is drawn away of his own lust, and enticed."

I Peter 1:6 – "Wherein you greatly rejoice, though now for a reason, if need be, you are in heaviness through manifold temptations:"

II Peter 2:9 – "The Lord knows how to deliver the godly out of temptations, and to reserve the unjust unto the Day of Judgment to be punished."

Jude 24 – "Now unto Him that is able to keep you from falling, and to present you faultless before the presence of His glory with exceeding joy."

TRUSTING

Psalm 5:11 – "But let all those that put their trust in you rejoice; let them ever shout for joy, because you defend them: let them also that love Your name be joyful in You."

Psalm 18:2 – "The Lord is my rock, and my fortress, and my deliverer; my God, my strength, in Whom I will trust; my buckler, and the horn of my salvation, and my high tower."

Psalm 37:5 – "Commit your way unto the Lord; trust also in Him; and He shall bring it to pass."

Proverbs 3:5, 6 – "Trust in the Lord with all your heart; and lean not unto your own understanding. In all Your ways acknowledge Him, and He shall direct Your paths."

Isaiah 12:2 – "Behold, God is my salvation; I will trust, and not be afraid: for the Lord Jehovah is my strength and my song; He also is become my salvation."

VICTORY

II Chronicles 32:8 – "With him is an arm of flesh; but with us is the Lord our God to help us, and to fight our battles. And the people rested themselves upon the words of Hezekiah king of Judah."

Romans 8:37 – "Nay, in all these things we are more than conquerors through Him that loved us."

I Corinthians 15:17 – "But thanks be to God, which gives us the victory through our Lord Jesus Christ."

II Corinthians 2:14 – "Now thanks be unto God, which always causes us to triumph in Christ, and makes manifest the savoir of his knowledge by us in every place."

II Timothy 2:19 – "Nevertheless the foundation of God stands sure, having this seal, The Lord knows them that are His. And, Let every one that names the name of Christ depart from iniquity."

I John 5:4 – "For whatsoever is born of God over comes the world: and this is the victory that overcomes the world, even our faith."

Revelation 3:5 – "He that overcomes, the same shall be clothed in white raiment; and I will not blot out his name out of the book of life, but I will confess his name before my Father, and before His angels."

Revelation 21:7 – "He that overcomes shall inherit all things; and I will be his God and he shall be My son."

JESUS CHRIST IS THE SAVIOUR OF THE WORLD

Matthew 1:21 – "And she shall bring forth a son, and you shall call His name Jesus, for He shall save His people from their sins."

Luke 19:10 – "For the Son of man is come to seek and to save that which was lost."

John 3:16 – "For God so loved the world, that He gave His only begotten Son, that whosoever believeth in Him should not perish, but have everlasting life."

John 14:6 – "Jesus say unto him, I am the way, the truth, and the life: no man comes unto the Father, but by me."

Acts 4:12 – "Neither is there salvation in any other; for there is none other name under heaven given among men, whereby we must be saved."

Romans 5:8 – "But God commends His love toward us, in that, while we were yet sinners, Christ died for us."

Ephesians 1:7 – "In whom we have redemption through His blood, the forgiveness of sins, according to the riches of His grace."

I John 5:12 – "He that has the Son has life; and he that has not the Son of God has not life."

ASSURANCE OF SALVATION

Matthew 24:5 – "Heaven and earth shall pass away, but my words shall not pass away."

John 5:24 – "Verily, verily, I say unto you, he that hears My Word and believes on Him that sent me, has everlasting life, and shall not come into condemnation; but is passed from death unto life."

John 6:37 – "All that the Father gives me shall come to me; and him that comes to me 1 will in no wise cast out."

John 10:28 – "And I give unto them eternal life, and they shall never perish; neither shall any man pluck them out of my hand."

John 20:32 – "But these are written that you might believe that Jesus is the Christ, the Son of God; and that believing you might have life through His name."

Romans 8:16 – "The Spirit itself bears witness with our spirit, that we are the children of God."

I John 5:13 – "These things have I written unto you that believe on the name of the Son of God, that you may know that you have eternal life."